ST

MEDITATIONS

MARCUS AURELIUS COMPLETE WORKS 1

Stoicism in Plain English

Dr Chuck Chakrapani

The Stoic Gym Publications

Stoic Gym Publications
www.thestoicgym.com

Stoic Foundations/Chuck Chakrapani. —1st ed.
ISBNs:
Print: 978-0-920219-48-5
ePub: 978-0-920219-49-2
Mobi: 978-0-920219-50-8
PDF: 978-0-920219-51-5
18 19 20 21 22 23 24 25 26   1 2 3 4 5 6 7 8 9 0

Contents

Stoic Meditations 1

1. Debts and Gratitude for Lessons Learned 5

2. Change is Nature's Way 17

3. Only the Present Matters 27

4. Universe is Change. Life is Opinion 39

5. Walk Your Path 59

6. Play Your Role in the World 77

7. Nature is Logical 97

8. Take Refuge in Your Inner Citadel 119

9. Get Your Good from Yourself 141

10. A Healthy Mind Can Face Anything 159

11. Learn the Art of Living 177

12. This is Your Moment 193

About the Author 213

Also by the Author 214

Stoic Meditations

This is the first of two books covering the complete works of Marcus Aurelius in plain English. This book by Emperor Marcus Aurelius (121 –180 CE) is one of the most beloved and widely read Stoic books. Aurelius wrote these notes to himself and not for general publication. Originally known as *To Himself*, they are now more widely known as *Meditations*.

In this book, I have followed the same format as the other titles in this *Stoicism in Plain English* series with two exceptions: the addition of chapter summaries and a difference from how Book 1 of Meditations is structured.

Chapter summaries

Unlike the other books in this series, this book does not contain chapter summaries. The main reason for this is that each chapter (or 'book'), except the first one, does not deal with a unified theme, as each chapter is Marcus Aurelius' thoughts as they came to him. He had no reason to organise his thoughts in any way since they were just his own thoughts and not meant for public consumption. Even the chapter titles that I have added are somewhat arbitrary. However, one can get an idea of what a chapter contains by simply reviewing the subtitles (added by me) in each 'book.'

A note on the structure of "Book 1"

In this Plain English series, I have tried to keep my rendering as close to the original as possible, so the reader not only knows what the Stoics said but also how they said it. However, for this first chapter (Book 1), I have somewhat deviated from the structure of the original text.

Here, Marcus Aurelius recalls the several lessons he learned over the years from different people with gratitude. Some lessons were taught directly to him while he learned others by observing the people he mentions. While Aurelius' prose here is clear, the paragraph structure he uses – describing the qualities of people in a paragraph format – often veils the lessons behind them. To make it easy to follow what lessons he learned from others, I have listed the lessons as bullet points, whether they were taught directly to him or through simple observations. I have also stated all lessons in the imperative style. My rationale for the revised structure is that it focuses on the lessons taught by different people to the exclusion of all else.

STOIC MEDITATIONS • 3

As Robin Hard[1] points out with each of Aurelius' paragraphs, we need to add the idea "From ... I have learned to value the following quality" or "I have received the following benefit."

BOOK 1

CHAPTER 2

Debts and Gratitude for Lessons Learned

The Background

It was the last decade of Marcus Aurelius' life. The Emperor was in Granua, fighting a war with the Quadi who lived in the Southern part of Bohemia and Moravia.

He reflects on his eventful life. He was not born into a royal family, yet was adopted by one. He did not want to be a ruler, yet he became one. He ruled the largest empire the world had ever know until that time, yet his empire was invaded from several fronts, and he spent much of his time in battlefields fighting invaders. He was kind and powerful, yet his wife was unfaithful, his son was incompetent, and his associates plotted against him. He could have chosen a life of extravagance and luxury like many of his predecessors, yet he chose a life driven by duty, forgiveness, and goodness.

As he looks back on his life and his few remaining years, he does not think about his own greatness or his achievements. He is neither regretful nor self-pitying. His first thoughts are about the many lessons he learned from many people – mostly by their example. He starts recording the lessons he learned from others, not for anyone to read but for his own benefit.

---

1. My grandfather Verus[2]

- Be courteous.
- Be of serene temper.

---

2. My father, from my memories and his reputation[3]

- Be manly, without being showy.

---

3. My mother[4]

- Be pious.
- Be generous.
- Avoid meanness in thoughts and actions.
- Lead a simple life, unlike the rich.

---

4. My great grandfather[5]

- Get a good private education, avoid public schools.
- Spend money on good education, without begrudging.

---

5. My first teacher[6]

- Don't support either side in a race or a fight.
- Don't be afraid of your own work.

- Limit your needs and attend to them.
- Mind your own business.
- Don't gossip.

---

6. Diognetus[7]

- Don't waste time on trivial things.
- Be sceptical of astrologers and fortune-tellers.
- Avoid distractions like cockfighting.
- Don't resent unwelcome truths.
- Study philosophy.
- Practice writing in early years.
- Practice a rigorous life of Greek disciplines – such as sleeping on a simple cot.

---

7. Rusticus[8]

- Train and discipline your character.
- Don't be side-tracked by other trivial pursuits.
- Don't write books on abstract questions or give moralising talks.
- Avoid composing imaginary descriptions of a *Simple Life* or a *Selfless Person*.
- Steer clear of oratory, poetry, and elegant writing.
- Don't dress up while relaxing at home.
- Write candidly.
- Be conciliatory if people who made you angry or upset you want to make it up to you.
- Read attentively, not superficially.

- Don't be taken in by smooth talkers.
- With thanks for introducing me to Epictetus' *Discourses* and even lending me his own copy.

---

8. Apollonius[9]

- Be independent (have inner freedom).
- Be decisive. Don't leave anything to chance.
- Pay attention to reason and to nothing else, even for a brief moment.
- Be the same always: whether going through intense pain, the loss of a child, or a chronic illness.
- Don't be irritable when you teach.
- Be energetic and yet relaxed.
- Learn how to accept apparent favours from friends without being disrespectful.

---

9. Sextus[10]

- Be kind.
- Rule your household with fatherly authority.
- Understand the real meaning of living according to nature.
- Be dignified without being self-conscious.
- Show good-natured concern for friends.
- Be patient with amateurs and dreamers.
- Be courteous to everyone (like Sextus who charmed everyone and yet commanded their complete respect.)
- Investigate and analyse the essential rules of life with understanding and logic.

- Never display anger or any kind of aggressive emotion.
- Be calm and full of kind affection.
- Praise quietly without fanfare.
- Don't parade your knowledge.

10. Alexander, the grammarian

- Avoid finding faults unnecessarily.
- Don't be a harsh critic. Don't correct people for their grammar, mispronunciation, or dialect. Instead, correct others' mistakes by indirect means such as using the right expressions yourself. Or, join the discussion and talk about the matter under consideration and not about diction. Or, use some other tactful method to suggest the right expression indirectly.

11. Fronto, my mentor[11]

- Recognize that absolute power produces malice, cunning, and hypocrisy.
- Recognize that "noble families" lack the feelings of ordinary humanity.

12. Alexander, the Platonist[12]

- Don't say or write constantly that you are too busy unless you need to.
- Don't avoid responsibilities to society on the excuse that you are too busy.

13. Catulus, the Stoic

- Don't make light of a friend's rebuke, even if it is not justified. Do your best to put things right.
- Speak respectfully of your teachers (as we read in the memoirs of Domitus and Athenodotus[13].) Love your children.

14. Seruus, my brother

- Love your family, truth, and justice.
- Through him, I came to know of Threasea, Cato, Helvidius, Dion, and Brutus[14] and learned that a community should be based on equality and freedom of speech for all. The job of the ruler is to ensure the liberty of his people.
- Have a fair and objective appreciation of philosophy.
- Be open-hearted and of even temper.
- Be confident that your friends love you.
- Be clear about your likes and dislikes with your friends and why you may disagree with them, but do it gently (as my brother did).

15. Maximus[15]

- Don't waver in your resolve.
- Be cheerful even in sickness and other misfortunes.

- Do your duties quietly and without complaining, while being dignified and charming (as Maximus was).
- Speak as you believe.
- Act as you judge right.
- Don't be bewildered or timid.
- Never be hasty or negligent or at a loss.
- Neither despair nor pretend to be happy.
- Don't let anger or jealousy have any power over you.
- Be kind, sympathetic, and sincere. Let your goodness be innate rather than coached.
- Don't let anyone make you feel inferior and give anyone any cause to challenge your integrity.
- Have a sense of humour.

---

16. Antoninus Pius, my adoptive father

- Be gentle.
- Stick to your thought-out decisions.
- Be indifferent to superficial honours.
- Work hard. Persevere.
- Be willing to listen to anyone who says anything for the common good.
- Reward people strictly based on their merit.
- Know when to push and when to back off.
- Do not pursue boys.
- Recognize that others have their own life. Friends have no obligation to dine with you or travel with

you. If they have other things to do, it should make no difference to you.

- Examine thoroughly and patiently every question that comes up in meetings. Don't be content with first impressions and be dismissive.
- Make your friendships long-lasting. Don't be arbitrary or extravagant.
- Always rise to the occasion.
- Be cheerful.
- Plan ahead and pay attention to every detail.
- Be attentive to the country's needs. Conserve resources and put up with the criticisms for doing so.
- Don't be superstitious before the gods.
- Don't curry favour or pander.
- Be calm, be steady. Look down upon anything flashy or faddish.
- Accept the comforts that come your way without reluctance or smugness. When they are there, use them; when they are not, have no regrets.
- Don't be misleading, glib, or obscure. Be mature and accomplished.
- Don't be influenced by flattery. Be qualified to govern yourself and others.
- Be respectful of true philosophers but don't be critical of others, even if you don't take their advice.
- When with others, be friendly, pleasant, and gracious, but don't flatter.

- Take reasonable care of your body. Don't be anxious about its appearance or about living long. Be mindful of it and look after yourself so well that your body hardly needs medical attention, drugs, or ointments.
- Don't be jealous but recognise people with outstanding abilities whatever field they come from – public speaking, law, ethics, or whatever. Rather, support them so they can fulfil their potential.
- Respect tradition but don't go looking for public recognition of it.
- Don't be restless and be pulled in all directions but be comfortable with your place and your pursuits.
- Quickly return to your regular work with vigour once your sickness is healed.
- Don't have personal secrets. Keep work-related secrets to a minimum.
- When you are involved in public actions (such as building projects or distributing money), be restrained and don't go looking for recognition.
- Don't bathe during strange hours. Don't build for the sake of vanity.
- Don't be critical of your food or the cut and colour of your clothes or the looks of people around you.
- Readily accept apologies. Let rudeness, harshness, and bullying be alien to you.

- Don't be angry or agitated. Approach everything calmly, methodically, decisively, and consistently.
- Know how to enjoy or avoid things (as Socrates did) that most people find hard to enjoy or stay away from. Being so strong to consent or refrain at the right time is the mark of an excellent and unconquerable soul (like the one exhibited by Maximus in his sick bed.)

---

17. The gods

I thank the gods

- For giving me good grandparents, good parents, a good sister, and, without exception, good teachers, comrades, relatives, and friends.
- For my never losing control with them, although, with my temperament, I could have easily done so. But, thanks to the gods, circumstances never came together in such a way to test me.
- For my not being raised with my grandfather's mistress long enough to lose my innocence.
- For my not being impatient to enter adulthood until it was time.
- For curing me of my arrogance and making me realise that one can live without a team of bodyguards, royal clothes, lamps, statues, and outward splendour. You can live like an ordinary person without losing your authority needed to carry out the affairs of the state.

- For giving me a brother[16] whose character constantly challenged my own. Yet, he was respectfully affectionate and warmed my heart.
- For giving me children who are neither stupid nor physically deformed.
- For limiting my talent in rhetoric, poetry, and similar subjects that might have absorbed my time, if I had found I had a talent for them.
- For [guiding me] to confer early the honours on people who brought me up they seemed to want, instead of delaying until they got older.
- For acquainting me with Apollonius, Maximus, and Rusticus.
- For showing me clearly and repeatedly the true inwardness of living in accordance with nature.
- For doing all they could – their favours, their help, and their inspiration – to make sure that I could live in accordance with nature. If I have not achieved that goal yet, it is not anyone's fault but my own; I didn't pay attention to their reminders – in fact, their directions were clear at every step.
- For my body that has survived my kind of life for so long.
- For (guiding me) not to touch a Benedicta or a Theodotus[17] and, even later, when I was overcome by passion, letting me recover unharmed. Although I had differences of opinion with Rusticus, I never did anything that I would have regretted later.

- For (letting) my mother spend her last years with me, even though she died young.
- For having the resources to help anyone in need and for not being in a position to need the help myself from others.
- For having a wife who is obedient, loving, and humble.
- For giving me competent tutors for my children.
- For prescribing remedies in my dreams for my ailments, especially coughing blood and dizziness, as it happened in Caieta and Chrysa.
- For not letting me fall into the hands of sophists when I got interested in philosophy. Or to get bogged down in writing books, logic-chopping, or natural science,
- For all these good things for which a human being needs the help of fortune and the gods.

Book 2

Change is Nature's Way

Still among the Quadis, the emperor continues recording his thoughts. He starts his morning meditation by reminding himself that others will be ungrateful, unreasonable, and unkind, but none of this should affect our goodness. We should be forgiving, rational, and, above all, kind towards everyone, especially the people who offend us. This theme that, no matter how someone behaves, it is our job to be good runs throughout the twelve books of Meditations.

1. Morning meditation

When you get up in the morning, tell yourself this. Today I will meet people who are interfering, ungrateful, arrogant, disloyal, jealous, and selfish. They are like this because they don't know what is good and what is evil. But I have seen the beauty of good and the ugliness of evil. I realise that the wrongdoer is my brother; not in a physical sense, but as a rational being who shares the divine with me. So, none of them can hurt me. No one can link me to what is ugly. I cannot be angry with my brother or hate him. We were born to work together, like two feet, two hands, eyelids, or upper and lower rows of teeth. To obstruct each other is unnatural. What is anger or hatred if not obstruction?

---

2. Pay attention to reason and reason only

What am I? A little flesh, a little breath, and a mind (the reasoning faculty) to rule all. Forget your books. It is not allowed. They are not a part of you.

- *Your flesh.* You are already close to death. Don't think of your flesh – its sticky blood, its bones, its network of nerves, veins, and arteries.
- *Your breath.* What is it? A whiff of wind. Not even the same wind but every moment puffed out and drawn again.
- *Your mind.* But the third, the mind (your reasoning faculty) is the master. You should focus on this.

You are an old man. Don't allow your mind to be slavish. Don't let your selfish impulses jerk you around like a puppet. Stop complaining about your fate, grumbling about today, and mistrusting tomorrow.

---

3. The universe is maintained by change

The divine is full of wisdom. Even the unpredictable chance has a place in nature. It is a part of the complex tapestry of things governed by wisdom. It is the source

STOIC MEDITATIONS • 19

of everything that flows. The needs of the world and the welfare of the universe are allied with it, and you are a part of it. Whatever nature does as a whole is good for every part of it.

The universe is maintained by change – both in the basic elements and the things created by them. Be content to know these. Hold them as the basic principles. Forget your quest for books. So, when the time comes to depart, you won't complain but meet it with good grace, and genuine gratitude to the gods.

4. Use your time wisely

Think. How many years you have been putting it off, how many times have the gods given you extensions and you ignored them. It is time that you recognised the nature of the universe, what power rules it and from what source you came from. You only have limited time. Use it then to advance your enlightenment. Or it will be gone, and you will have no power over it.

5. Pay attention to what is at hand

Every minute of the day, do what is in front of you with precision, natural dignity, humanity, independence, and justice. Do it like a Roman. Do it like a human being. Free yourself from all other distractions. You can do it if you do everything as if it were the last act of your life.

Dismiss random thoughts.

Don't let passion overcome reason.

Don't try to impress others.
Don't be self-absorbed or be discontent.
See, how little you have to master to let days flow in quietness and piety? All you need to do is follow a few precepts. The gods ask nothing more of you.

---

6. Don't look for others' approval

My soul, you are doing wrong to yourself. Your chance to set it right will be over altogether too soon. Human beings have only one life. Yours is already coming to an end. And yet, you are looking for happiness in other people's approval rather than trusting your own honour.

---

7. Know how to be quiet and focus your thoughts

Do external things bother you? Then take time to be quiet and strengthen your knowledge of the good. Calm your restlessness. Also guard yourself against another error – wasting all your life by being busy but have no idea how to direct your efforts or focus your thoughts.

---

8. To be happy, pay attention to your soul

You won't come to grief if you ignore what happens in other people's souls. But if you don't keep track of what happens in your own soul, you can't avoid unhappiness.

STOIC MEDITATIONS • 21

9. Remember the nature of the world and your nature

If you remember the nature of the world, your nature, how you relate to the world – such a small part relating to such a large one – no one can stop you from being in accordance with nature, both in word and in action.

10. Sins of desire are worse than of anger

In comparing sin (to the extent it is possible to do so), Theophrastus[18] says that the sins committed out of desire are worse than the ones committed out of anger. The angry person turns his back on reason because of discomfort and perceived constraint. But the person motivated by desire, whose main motive is pleasure, is more self-indulgent and less manly.

Both in theory and in practice, then, the sin that is committed in search of pleasure deserves a harsher rebuke than a sin that is committed out of pain. The angry person is more like someone without choice, overcome by a sudden loss of self-control. But the person motivated by an eagerness to satisfy their desire does so by choice.

11. You have the power to avoid harm

In everything you say and think, remember this. It is in your hands when you want to leave this life. If the gods exist, then leaving the human state is nothing to be afraid of. They will not subject you to harm. If they don't exist or don't care what happens to us, what's the point of living in a world without gods or Providence? But they do exist. They do care for what happens to us. They have given us the full power we need to avoid harm. If there were anything harmful in life's other experiences, they would give us the power to avoid those too.

But how can something that does not damage your character damage you? Nature would not have been so ignorant as to overlook dangers of this kind or, seeing the danger, powerless to prevent or correct them. Neither would it make a mistake, through a lack of power or skill, of letting good and bad things happen to people indiscriminately, whether they are virtuous or not.

Yet, living and dying, honour and dishonour, pain and pleasure, riches and poverty and the like happen to good and bad people alike. These things neither elevate us nor degrade us. So, they are neither good nor evil.

---

12. Death is natural and necessary

We have the mental powers help us see how quickly things vanish – objects in space and memory in time. We should observe the real nature of things our senses experience. They attract us with pleasure, or frighten us with pain, or are boldly encouraged by pride. How cheap, contemptible, grimy, decaying, and dying they all are! We should understand the true worth of those whose voices and opinions create a reputation.

We should also understand the nature of death. Only when we steadily think about it and break down our imaginary ideas about it, will we realise that it is nothing but a process of nature. Only children will be afraid of it. In fact, it is not just a process, but a necessary one. We can learn how human beings have contact with God, with what part, and what happens to that part when they die.

13. Your good is not outside of you

Nothing is more pathetic than people running around trying to understand what is behind creation and how to get a glimpse into other people's souls. They don't realise that holding on to the divine in them and serving it loyally is all they need. Serving means keeping away from passion, from aimlessness, and from being discontented with nature, divine or human. What is divine deserves our reverence for its excellence. What is human deserves our goodwill because it is like us; it also deserves our pity at times because of our ignorance of good and evil – a disability as crippling as the inability to distinguish black from white.

14. The present moment is all that you own

Even if you live three thousand – or thirty thousand – years, you should remember this. You cannot lose any other life than the one you are living now. And you can have no other life than the one you are losing. The longest life is the same as the shortest life. The present moment is the same for everyone. Once you lose it, it is not yours anymore. Your loss is limited to this one fleeting moment. No one can lose what is already past and what is yet to be. How could you lose what you don't have?

Remember two things.

i.   All things have always been the same and are repeated over and over again. It makes no difference whether they are repeated every hundred years, two hundred years, or forever.

ii. When the longest-lived person and the shortest-lived person die, they lose exactly the same thing. All you can lose is the present moment. This is all you own, and you cannot lose what you don't own.

---

15. Things are what we think they are

People object to Monimus the Cynic's[19] saying "Things are what we think they are," but if you see the truth behind it, you will see its value.

---

16. Five ways a soul can harm itself

The soul inflicts on itself the greatest harm when it becomes a tumour on the universe. Nature is a collection of the nature of all things.

• So, when you quarrel with your circumstances, you rebel against nature.

- A second harm is to reject your fellow human being and treat them with malice, as one might do when angry.
- A third, to give in to pleasure and pain.
- A fourth, to put on an act and be insincere and false, either in word on in deed.
- A fifth, to act aimlessly and waste energy, without thinking and without a purpose. Even the smallest of our actions should have a purpose. The goal of rational beings is to follow the law of the primal communities and states.

---

17. Constant change is nature's way

Your time is just a moment. You are constantly changing. Your senses are dimming. Your body is decaying. Your soul is spinning around. Your fortune is unpredictable. And your fame is doubtful. In short, your body is like a river. Your soul is like a dream and mist. Life is warfare, a brief journey to an alien land. After fame, obscurity.

Where can you find the power to protect and guide your way? In only one thing: philosophy. To be a philosopher means

- Making sure that the power within is safe, free from attacks, and above pain and pleasure.
- Doing nothing aimlessly, falsely, or dishonestly.
- Not depending on someone doing something or not doing something.
- Welcoming whatever happens as coming from the same source as itself.

- Above all, accepting death cheerfully, as nothing more than the elements you are made of simply dissolving. If the elements themselves are not harmed by change, why should we be afraid of all of them changing and separating? It is the nature's way, and there's no evil in it.

BOOK 3

Only the Present Matters

In the spring of 170 CE, hordes of German warrior bands attacked Roman provinces along the Danube River. Carnuntum, together with the Viennese basin, was overrun in the Marcomannic invasion. Marcus Aurelius began his counteroffensive from this spot. For two years (172-74), Carnuntum was his headquarters. Here the emperor starts writing the third book of his Meditations.

1. The grace and charm of nature

As our life is wearing away every day, less and less of it remains. That's not the only thing to think about. Even if we live longer, it is doubtful if our mind will continue to understand the world, or if it will have the capacity to contemplate so it can understand things that are divine and human.

When you start to become senile, you may still breathe well, eat well, feel well, and imagine well. But the ability to use all your mental powers, to calculate where your duty lies, to face problems that arise, whether it is time to call it quits, or to make any other decisions that need your intellect, begin to slow down. So, we must hurry, not because every hour we are closer to death but because, even before death, our perception and understanding start going down. We should also remember the casual grace and charm of nature.

- A loaf of bread splits open in the oven; random cracks appear on it. These unintended flaws are right and sharpen our appetite.
- Figs, when they ripen, also crack open.
- Olives, when they are about to fall just before they decay, appear more beautiful.
- So are drooping stalks of wheat, the wrinkling skin of a staring lion, foam from a wild boar's mouth, and many more such sights.

There is nothing beautiful about these sights when we see them in isolation. Yet, due to some other process of nature, they become charming and attractive.

---

2. The incredible beauty of nature

Almost everything – even if it is only incidental to something else – adds extra pleasure to someone who is sensitive and insightful about how the universe works.

The grinning jaws of lions and tigers are as admirable as paintings or sculptures of them. So is the mature beauty of an old man or an old woman, and the loveliness of children. Things like these will not appeal to everyone, but the person who has developed a real friendship with nature and her works will be fascinated.

3. Death is natural

Hippocrates cured many illnesses, but fell ill and died. The Chaldeans [Babylonian astrologers] predicted the death of many, but eventually, they died too. Alexander, Pompey, and Julius Caesar completely destroyed cities, slaughtered thousands of foot-soldiers and horsemen in battle, but when the time came, they too passed away. Heraclitus [thinker, 6th Century CE] told us again and again that the universe will end in fire, but it was water that saturated his body, and he died in a dung heap. Democritus was killed by vermin and Socrates by a vermin of another kind.

So?

This. You get on board, go on a voyage, and reach the port. Time to get off. Is it into another life? If so, there are gods even there. Is it into nothingness? Then you won't be in the clutches of pleasure and pain; you won't be controlled by your body, which is inferior to what it serves. One is mind and spirit; the other is clay and garbage.

4. Let all your thoughts be simple and kind

Don't waste the rest of your life worrying about others, unless it is for some mutual benefit. The time you spend wondering what so-and-so is doing, saying, thinking, or plotting is the time that's lost for some other task.

So, see to it that your train of thoughts is not idle or random and certainly not inquisitive or malicious. Your thoughts should be such that if someone asks "What's on your mind?", you should be able to answer frankly and without hesitation. This would prove that all your thoughts are simple and kindly. They would be the thoughts of a social being, one unconcerned with pleasure and pain, jealousy, envy, suspicion, or any other sentiment you would be ashamed to admit.

Someone like that – determined and aiming for higher things – is like a priest and minister of the gods. He is making full use of his inner power that can keep him unblemished by pleasure, unaffected by pain, untouched by guilt, and unmoved by evil, a competitor in the greatest of all contests – mastering passions. He is through and through honest, and welcoming of whatever comes his way, never worrying about what others say, do, or think about him, unless it is in the public interest.

He minds his own business paying attention only to his own role in the universe. He keeps his actions honourable and believes that everything happens for the best. The fate that directs us is directed by something above it.

He keeps in mind that all human beings are related, that caring for others is part of being human. He does not follow everyone's opinions, but only of those whose lives conform to nature. The lives of others are in disorder. They exhibit this both at home and abroad, by night and by day, and by the company they keep. He doesn't care for their approval. They can't even meet their own standards.

---

5. How to act

- Act willingly and quickly, taking into account common interest.
- Act deliberately – yet without wavering
- Avoid pretentious over-refinement.
- Avoid talkativeness and self-importance.
- Let your spirit represent a human being, a Roman, a ruler.
- Hold your ground like a soldier. Wait patiently for a recall signal from the battlefield of life. Be ready to welcome the signal. Let your credit need no guarantee from you or from others.
- This is the secret of cheerfulness – not depending on someone's help or expecting them to provide us tranquillity.
- We have to stand up straight, not be propped up to stand up straight.

---

6. Make up your mind and hold your ground

If you find something in your life that is
- better than justice, truth, self-control, and courage,
- better than basing your actions on reason resulting in peace of mind, and

- better than accepting what is beyond your control,

then embrace it wholeheartedly and without reservation. Rejoice in what you found.

But, if you find nothing superior to the spirit that lives within you, directing your impulses, judging every impression, and avoiding physical temptations (as Socrates would say), declaring allegiance to the gods and compassion for humankind; if you find nothing else to be more important or more valuable than that, then leave no room in your life to go after rival pursuits. Because, once you falter and lose your way, you will no longer be able to devote yourself completely to this ideal you have chosen. Ambitions of a different nature cannot compete for the title of goodness, which belongs only to reason and civic duty – not to the applause of others, power, or self-indulgence. It may all seem compatible with goodness for a while, but soon enough they will gain the upper hand and throw you off-balance. So make your choice, simply and voluntarily. Choose what is best and stick to it.

You may say, "Best is what benefits me." If it is best for you as a reasonable being, then do hold on to it, but if it is best for you as an animal, then say so, and stand your ground without being a show-off. Just make sure that you have considered your views fully.

7. Have the highest regard for your mind

Never believe that something is doing you good if it makes you betray a trust, lose self-respect, be hateful or suspicious, subject to ill will or insincerity, or do something behind closed doors. If you have the highest regard for your mind, the divinity and the service of goodness, you will not be pretentious or complaining. You will seek neither solitude nor company. Best of all, you will be free of fear and desire. You will not care whether the soul housed in your body is yours to keep for a short or a long time. If it is time for you to go, you will go as willingly as you do anything else, with grace and honour. You will have no other care in your life except to keep your mind from wandering into paths unsuitable for an intelligent and social being.

8. Disciplined and purified mind – a portrait

When your mind is disciplined and purified, there is no hint of corruption, no unclean spot, no rotting sore. Fate cannot snatch you away before you are fulfilled. It would be like an actor walking away in the middle of a performance before the play is finished. You are neither grovelling nor arrogant. You are neither dependent on others nor avoid them. Although answerable to no one, you are not evasive.

9. Respect your ability to form a judgment

Treat with respect your ability to form a judgement. That's what protects your mind from forming opinions contrary to nature and contrary to reason. It's what makes you careful, sociable, and conforming to the will of the divine.

10. Only the present moment matters

Let go of everything else. Just remember the following few truths.

- You only live in the present, this fleeting moment. The rest of your life is already gone or not yet revealed.
- Your life is a little thing, lived in a corner of the world.
- The longest fame is also little, dependent on people who themselves pass away. They don't know even their own lives, let alone the lives of people who are long dead.

11. Examine the nature of what you perceive

Add one more maxim to the above. When you see something, try to understand and define what it is, even if it is just an outline. This will help you to know what it really is – by stripping its attributes to find its true nature, to know what it is and what it is made of, what it will become once again.

Examine every life experience logically and accurately. It will expand your mind like nothing else. Find out where it belongs, what its purpose is, what role it plays in the universe, and its value to human beings as citizens of that supreme city – the city in which all other cities are households.

For example, what is this thing that is producing an impression upon me right now? What is it made of? How long is it designed to last? What response does it ask of me – gentleness, courage, honesty, good faith, sincerity, self-reliance, or some other quality? In each case, learn to say,

"This comes from God," or

"This comes from the complex weavings of fate," or

"This comes from a human being who is made of the same elements as me, and so related to me, but does not know what nature requires of them."

But I do. Therefore, I will deal with this person as nature asks of me – with kindness and fairness. When it is not a question of good or evil, I will treat it as it deserves.

---

12. Towards the good life

If you do what is in front of you with reason, enthusiasm, and energy – and yet with humanity – free from distractions, keeping your inner spirit pure and straight as if you have to give it back any moment, and if you steadily hold on to this without wavering, doing every action in conformity with nature, saying every word truthfully and fearlessly, then the good life will be yours. No one can hold you back.

13. The human and the divine are intertwined

Doctors keep their scalpels and other instruments ready at hand for emergencies. Likewise, keep your principles always ready to understand both human and divine. Even in your smallest action, don't forget the intimate link between the two. Nothing human can be done without the divine. Nothing divine can be done without the human.

14. Don't delude yourself

Don't kid yourself. You are not going to read these notebooks again, or the history of Greeks and Romans, or any of the books you have set aside to read in your old age. Write off your empty hopes and race to the finish line. If you have any regard for your well-being, look after its security while you still can.

15. Understand the significance of words

People don't realise the full meaning of words like 'stealing,' 'sowing,' 'buying,' 'being peaceful,' and 'seeing one's duty' (which needs a different kind of seeing).

16. What is different about a good person?

Body, soul, and mind. The body for sensation. The soul for action. The mind for reasoning.

The capacity for sensation belongs even to wild animals, to Nero or to Phalaris[20].

Even people who deny the gods, betray their country, and do things behind closed doors have minds to guide them to the clear path of duty.

If all else is common to all, what is different about a good person?

- Welcoming whatever happens.
- Not defiling the divine spirit within or disturb it with false beliefs but keep it serene, calmly obeying God.
- Saying only what is true.
- Doing only what is just.

She does not take offence at the world if it does not acknowledge her simple, modest, and cheerful life. She follows it steadily until it ends in purity, serenity, acceptance – in perfect and natural unity with what must be.

BOOK 4

Universe is Change. Life is Opinion

1. Inward power overcomes obstacles

Our inward power, when it is true to nature, will easily adjust itself to possibilities and opportunities that come our way. It doesn't need anything special. In seeking its aim, it is willing to compromise. It turns obstacles into fuel for its use. While a little lamp would be put off by rubbish thrown at it, a blazing fire consumes it and burns brighter.

2. Do things the right way

Don't act randomly. Do things the right way by understanding the principles behind them.

3. Universe is change. Life is opinion

People try to retreat to the country, to the beach, or the mountains. You wish you could do it too, but such fantasies are not worthy of a philosopher. Any moment you choose, you can retire within yourself. Nowhere can you go which is more peaceful and more untroubled than your soul. If you have developed all the resources within yourself, all you need is to contemplate to secure ease of mind or harmony. Make use of this retreat often and keep renewing yourself. Make the rules of life brief but profound. Practising them often will get rid of all aggravations, and you will return to your duties as you should, without complaining. Besides, what is there to complain about?

People's vices?

Remember these.

- We are all created for one another.
- Patience is a part of justice.
- No one chooses to be evil.
- Many of those who have feuded, envied, hated, and fought are now dead and buried.

So, stop fretting.

The role you are assigned in the world?

Then remember this dilemma. If it is not a wise Providence, then it is a mere jumble of atoms. Think of all the evidence for seeing the world as a city.

Your body?

Remember, all that body has to do is to detach itself and capture its own powers. Then it won't be involved in ordinary life – rough or smooth. Remember all that you have learned and accepted about pleasure and pain.

Your reputation?

Think how soon it will all be forgotten in the big hole of eternity before us and behind us! Note how erratic and arbitrary are those who praise us and how hollow the sound of their applause is. The entire world is just a point in space, and you live in an insignificant corner of it. Your fame is confined to this tiny area. How many here will praise you, and who are they?

Remember, then, to take refuge in yourself. Above all, don't strain and don't struggle. Be a master of yourself. See life as a person, as a human being, as a citizen, as a mortal. Among the many truths you need to think about often are these two.

i.   Things can never touch the soul. They stand out-side it, unmoving. Worry and anxiety come only from our inner perception.

ii.   Everything you see will soon change and will be no more. Think about the many changes you have already seen.

The whole universe is change. Life is just opinion.[21] [It is what you think it is.]

---

4. Everything has a source

Intelligence is common to all human beings. So is reason, which makes us rational beings. If this is so, reason tells all of us what to do and what not to do. This means we share a common law, which, in turn, makes us all fellow citizens. The world then is a single city.

Can there be any other basis for common citizenship? It is from this that we all share the same thought, reason, and law. Where else could they come from? The earthly elements you are made of come from the earth, the water from some other element, your breath from another source, and the heat and fire from theirs. Nothing can come from, or go back to, nothing. So our intelligence has to come from somewhere as well.

5. Death and birth are nature's mysteries

Death, like birth, is one of nature's mysteries. The same elements combine and then move apart. There is no shame in this. It doesn't contradict the plan of creation.

6. Don't wish for things contrary to reality

A person of a given nature will do things of a certain kind. That's the way it is. To wish otherwise is like wishing a fig tree not to produce its bitter juice. In any case, soon enough, he and you will be dead and soon be forgotten.

7. Don't harbour a sense of injury

Forget the belief "I've been harmed," and you won't feel harmed. Reject your sense of injury, and the injury itself disappears.

8. What cannot corrupt you, cannot corrupt your life

What cannot corrupt you, cannot corrupt your life. It cannot damage you inside or out.

9. Everything happens for the collective good

What happened had to have happened for the good of all.

10. Whatever happens, happens justly

Whatever happens, happens justly. Watch closely and you will see this is true. It is not just sequence of cause and effect but a sequence that is just and right – as if what is due is given out by a hand. Be as watchful as when you started and show goodness in all your actions. Continue to do so in all your actions.

11. Look at things as they really are

Don't imitate the opinions of the arrogant and don't let them dictate. Look at things as they really are.

12. Always think of the common good

You need two kinds of readiness.
i. To do only what reason tells us is for the common good; and

ii. To reconsider your position, when someone corrects you and shows that your judgment is incorrect. But, you should do so only when you believe that it is right and will benefit others. This must be the only reason, not pleasure or popularity.

13. Use your reason

"Do you have a reasoning faculty?"
"I do."
"Then why not use it? If reason does what it is supposed to do, what more do you want?"

14. You will return to your source

You are a part of the whole. You will become a part of what created you. Or, rather, you will be transformed into the creative reason of the universe, from which everything springs.

15. Everything ends sooner or later

Many lumps of incense fall from the same altar. Some sooner, some later. It makes no difference.

16. Rediscover the principles

Those who see you now as a monkey or an animal will be calling you a god within a week. All you have to do is rediscover your principles and reverence for reason.

17. You don't have a lot of time

Don't live as though there are a thousand years ahead of you. Death is at your elbow. Be good while you are still alive and able.

18. Do not look for faults in other people

If you do not worry about what others think, say, or do, but only about whether your actions are just and godly, you will gain time and tranquillity. Don't look for faults in others. Run straight towards your goal without looking left or right

19. Posthumous fame is meaningless

People want to be famous after their death. They forget that those who remember them will die soon too. And so will those who come after them. This will continue until your memory, passed to one another like a flame, is gone out forever.

Suppose that those who remember you live forever and your memory continues to live on. What is it to you? When you are in your grave, it means nothing. Even when you are alive, what good is praise except perhaps make your life a little more comfortable? You are rejecting what nature has given you today if you are concerned about what people say about you tomorrow.

20.   True beauty needs no praise

Anything that is beautiful in any way derives its beauty from itself and is complete in itself. Praise is not a part of it. Nothing is made better or worse by praise. This applies to even mundane things – such as natural objects or works of art.

Does true beauty need anything more? Certainly not, not any more than law, truth, kindness, or modesty. Can any of these things be made better by praise? Or made worse by criticism? Does the emerald lose its beauty if nobody admires it? Does gold, ivory, or purple? Does a lyre, a knife, a rosebud, or a bush?

21. What happens to souls after death?

If the soul survives after death, how did the air above find room for all of them since time began? How did the earth find room for all the bodies buried since the beginning of time? They stay for a while, change, and decompose to make room for other bodies.

Similarly, souls linger for a while and then change – they are diffused and then transformed into fire and then back into the creative principle of the universe, thus making room for other souls. This is what someone who believes in the survival of souls would say.

But, we should not just think of *buried* bodies. We consume many of them daily. So do other animals. How many bodies are swallowed up this way, buried in the bodies nourished by them! Yet there is room for all of them. They are converted into flesh and blood and transformed into air and fire. All the space needed thus becomes available.

How do we know all this is true?

By distinguishing between matter and cause.

22. Don't be carried away by impulse

Don't be swept off your feet. When you have an impulse, see if it is just. See things as they are.

23. Be in tune with the world and with nature

O world, I am in tune with every note of your harmony. Nothing is late for me, nothing is early for me, if it is the right time for you.

O nature, all your seasons bring me fruit. All things are from you, in you, and to you.

The poet says "Dear city of Cecrops.[22]" Can't we say at least "Dear city of God"?

24. Eliminate the non-essentials

The sage says "If you want to be content, do less." Even better, only do the essential, as demanded by reason in social being. Doing a few essential things and doing them well brings contentment.

Most of what we say and do is not essential. You will save time and trouble by eliminating it. At every step, ask yourself "Is this really necessary?" We need to eliminate not only idle actions but idle impressions as well. Then you won't act unnecessarily.

25. How capable are you of being a good person?

Test yourself. Are you capable of being a good person, a person who is content with your part in the universe, who wants to be just in what you do, and charitable in your ways?

26.Life is short. Seize every hour

You have seen all that [unpleasant things]. Now, look at this. Your part is to be serene, to be simple. Anyone who does wrong does wrong to himself. Has something happened to you? Good. It was supposed to happen. It was so decided when time began. It was woven into the pattern that is special to you, like everything else that happens. Life is short. Get as much as you can from each passing hour. Obey reason, be just. Be flexible, but be moderate.

27. The universe is orderly

The universe is either all order or all random and disorderly mishmash. How can there be order in you if the universe (of which you are a part) is disorderly? Things are different, dispersed, and interconnected. And yet there is oneness of feeling among all parts of nature.

28. A dark heart

A dark heart is unmanly, stubborn. The heart of an animal, a beast of the field, is childish, stupid, and false. A huckster's heart. A tyrant's heart.

29. Understand how the universe works

If you don't know what is in the universe, or how it works, you are stranger here. You are an exile. You have banished yourself from the state of reason.

You are blind. Your eyes of understanding have gone dark. You are a pauper, dependent on others, without any means of supporting yourself.

You are a blot on the world when you detach yourself from the laws of our common nature by refusing to accept what life assigns to you. (After all, this is what gave birth to you in the first place.) You are a limb cut off from the community when you cut off your soul from the single soul of all rational beings.

30.   Cling to reason

One philosopher has no books, another, no clothes. A third, only partly dressed, says, "Bread have I none, yet still I cling to reason." With nothing to show for my reading, I too cling to reason.

31. You're no one's master, no one's slave

Give your heart to the trade you have learned. Draw energy from it. Spend the rest of your days fully committed to the gods. You are no one's master and no one's slave.

32. Don't waste time on insignificant things

Think of the time Vespasian was in power. What do you see? Men and women marrying, bringing up children, getting sick, dying, waging war, throwing parties, doing business, farming, flattering, boasting, envying, scheming, cursing, complaining about their lives, loving, putting money away, seeking high offices and power. None of it survived.

Now move forward to the time of Trajan. It is the exact same life. All that is gone too.

Take a look at the records of other ages and people. See how all of them, after struggling for a while, passed away and became the elements that made them. More importantly, look at the list of people you know yourself. Those who pursued their own pride, and failed to do what they should have done, finding satisfaction in it.

When you find things like these, remember this. The effort you put into going after something should be in proportion to its worth. If you don't want to be discouraged, don't give more time than they deserve for insignificant things.

33. Everything passes. Accept what happens

Words once in common use have now gone out of use. What were household names once are now old-fashioned: Camilius, Caseo, Volesus, Dentatus, Scipio, Cato, Augustus, Hadrian, and Antoninus. All things fade into legend and are, in a little while, forgotten. Even glorious lives end this way. As for others, the moment their breath goes out, they are invisible and just hearsay.

After all, what is immortal fame?

An empty thing.

What should we aspire for?

This and only this. Just thought, unselfish action, truthful speech, acceptance of whatever happens as predestined and expected and coming from the same source.

34.   Let whatever happens happen

Gracefully hand yourself to Clotho (who spins the thread of life as one of the three Fates). Let her spin your thread out of the material of her choice.

35. We remember. We are remembered

Our lives are short. We remember. Then we are remembered.

36.   Change gives birth to all things

Notice how change gives birth to all things. Know that nature is happiest when things change to become new things. Whatever is now carries the seed of what is to come from it. A philosopher should know that the seeds that make plants or children are not the only seeds.

37. Justice is the only wisdom

Very soon, you will be dead. Even so, you are not single-minded and peaceful. You are still afraid that others can harm you. You are not yet giving. You are not yet convinced that justice is the only wisdom.

38.   Observe the wise

Carefully observe – what guides the actions of the wise? What do they do? What do they not do?

39.   Harm can only come from your thinking

What others think cannot harm you. Your changing body cannot harm you. Then what can? The part of your mind that judges what harms you. Refuse to accept its judgment and everything will be all right.

Even if its close neighbour – your body – is stabbed and burnt, aggravated, or degraded, let that judgment keep quiet. What happens to everyone – whether good or bad, whether they live in accordance with nature or

STOIC MEDITATIONS • 53

not – can neither be good nor bad. It neither helps nature's intentions nor hinders them.

40.   The intricate web of the universe

Think of the universe as one living organism made of a single substance and a single soul. Observe how everything feeds into that single experience of the whole, how everything moves with a single impulse, and how everything plays a part in everything that happens. See how intricate the coil is and how complex the web is.

41. Your soul, burdened by a body

Remember what Epictetus said: "A poor soul burdened with a corpse!"

42.   Change is neither good nor bad

There is nothing bad in undergoing change. Nothing good either.

43.   The river of time flows constantly

Time is a river. It is the irresistible flow of everything that is created. You glimpse something, and it is already carried past you and a new thing comes into sight. It is swept away quickly as well.

44.   Everything is normal and expected

Everything that happens is as normal and as expected as the rose in spring or the fruit in summer. This is true of disease, death, slander, conspiracy, and all other things that delight or trouble foolish people.

45.   Events are not random

What follows is closely linked to what happened before. Events are not random happenings with an order imposed on them, but are logically connected. Not only is what exists now ordered and harmonious, but things that come into being also show the same marvel. It is not mere sequence, but astonishing harmony.

46.   Don't blindly follow maxims

Remember the sayings of Heraclitus:

- Death of earth, the birth of water. Death of water, the birth of air. From air, fire. So round and round again.
- They have no clue as to where the road is leading.
- They are at odds with their own closest companion [the controlling Reason of the universe].
- They face this every day, yet they find it alien.
- We should not speak or act like those who are asleep (as people do when they dream).

- We should not speak or act like children who copy the words of their parents. (Don't blindly follow traditional maxims.)

47. Put your life in perspective

Suppose that a god tells you that you are going to die tomorrow or the day after. Unless you are a total coward, you will not argue about which day it should be. What difference between the two days? Now recognise that the difference between tomorrow and years later is just as trivial.

48. Nothing lasts for long

Now dead.

Think of the doctors who furrowed their brows over their ailing patients.

Think of the astrologers who predicted the death of others.

Think of the philosophers who talked endlessly about death and immortality.

Think of the warriors who killed one thousand people.

Think of the tyrants who abused the power of life and death over others with such terrible arrogance, as if they themselves couldn't die.

Think of the whole cities that perished: Helike, Pompeii, Herculaneum, and countless others.

Recall, one by one, the people you know yourself. One buried another, and that person was buried by a third and so on – all in a short time span.

See how fleeting and trivial life is. Yesterday a drop of semen, tomorrow a handful of ashes.

Therefore, spend your brief life as nature asks you to. Then go to your rest with good grace. Like the ripe olive falling as a blessing for the earth and a thanksgiving for the tree.

---

49. Be the rock. Let the waves crash

Be the rock over which waves keep crashing. It stands firm until the raging of the sea around it falls silent. Don't say "How unlucky that this has happened to me!" Say instead "How lucky that this has left me without bitterness, not upset by the present, not afraid the future!" This could have happened to anyone, but not everyone would have come out of the experience without feeling bitter. Why call the one unfortunate and the other fortunate? Can you call anything at all a misfortune if it doesn't violate nature's will? Well, now you are aware of nature's will. Does this thing that happened keep you from being just, generous, moderate, discreet, truthful, self-respecting, independent, and all else that allows you to act in accordance with nature? So remember this when you are tempted to feel bitter: What happened is no misfortune. To face it and succeed is good fortune.

50.   All lives are short in the infinite time

If you want to disregard death, think about those who greedily hang on to their life. How are they any better off than those who died young? In every case, in some place, at some time, they all are covered by dust – Caedicianus, Fabius, Julian, Lepidus, and the rest. They saw so many burials, only to be buried in turn.

Brief is our lifetime. And to live under these conditions, with these people, and in this miserable body? Don't get excited about it. Look at the abyss of time past and the infinity yet to come. When you look at all this, what more is Nestor (who lived to be very old) than a three-day-old baby?

51. Let your word and deed be sound

Run the short way. The short way is the way of nature. Perfecting the soundness of each word and deed is the goal. Follow that and you will be free of anxiety and stress, compromise, and pretension.

BOOK 5

Walk Your Path

1. Morning thoughts

When you wake up, unwilling to get out of bed, say to yourself:

I am born to do the work of a human being. What do I have to complain about if this is what I was born for? Or did I come into this world to lie in bed, covered in blankets?

"Ah, but this is much more pleasant!"

Were you born just feel pleasant and not for work, not for effort? Look at the plants, the birds, the ants and spiders and bees all busy doing their work, doing their part in the scheme of things. Are you unwilling to do your job as a human being? Do you refuse to do your part in nature's order?

"But I have to sleep some time."

Absolutely. But nature has set limits on that, in the same way it did on eating and drinking. You are crossing those limits and you are over-indulging. However, when it comes to working, you are well below what you could achieve.

You don't love yourself enough. If you did, you'd love your nature and what it asks of you. People who love what they do spend a lot of time doing it, even forgetting to wash or eat. You have less respect for your nature than an engraver has for engraving, the dancer for dancing, the miser for money, and the self-absorbed person for status. When they are really involved in their profession, they are ready to sacrifice eating and sleeping than to stop what they do. Is being a part of a community less valuable to you? Is it not worth your effort?

---

2. Be at peace

Set aside and forget every annoyance, distraction, and false impression. Be at peace. Totally.

---

3. Follow your nature

Any action or saying that is in accordance with nature is right for you. Don't be put off by other people's comments and criticism. If something is good, don't give up your right to it. Those who criticise you have their own motives and impulses. Don't be distracted by them, but keep your eyes straight ahead and follow your own nature and the nature of the world. (Their paths are the same.)

4. Walk the path until your last breath

I travel the roads of nature until it is time for me to lie down and rest. I give my last breath to the source of all my breaths and sink down upon this earth. It is from here my father derived his seed, my mother her blood, my nurse the milk. It is this earth that gave me food and drink all these years. It is greatly abused, but still allows me to walk on it.

5. Virtues need no aptitude to acquire

All right, you will never be known for your quick-wit. Still, there are plenty of other things left for which you can't claim to have no talent. Practice these things because they are totally in your power: sincerity, dignity, diligence, and moderation. Avoid grumbling. Be careful, considerate, and open. Speak and behave modestly. Carry yourself with authority. See how many qualities can be yours right now!

You say that you have no inborn capacity or aptitude for them, yet you continue to linger on a lower plane. Is it any lack of natural capacity that makes you quarrelsome, mean, fawning, railing at your health, cringing, bragging, and moody? Most certainly not. You could have got rid of these a long time ago. At worst, you may be called slow-witted and even this you can correct with practice, if you are not proud of it and try to make a virtue of your dullness.

6. Serve others without looking for credit

Some people will take quick credit for any service they provide you. Other people may not go that far, but will still consider you to be in their debt and be fully conscious of their service to you.

There are also people who don't at all think about what they have done – like the vine that produces grapes and looks for no more thanks. Like a horse that has just run a race. Like a dog that finished hunting. Like a bee that has stored honey.

We should be like them. We should not be thinking or talking about it, but move on to the next thing, just as the vine goes on to bearing the next season's grapes.

"Do you mean to say that we should be conscious of the things you mentioned?"

"Exactly. Yet we should be aware of our intentions, as they are the mark of a social being."

"But then shouldn't society also be aware of it?"

"True. But you miss my meaning, and you put yourself in the same class of people I described earlier who are misled by this kind of false logic. Understand the true meaning, and you will never have to worry about neglecting your social duty."

7. Keep your prayers simple and innocent

The Athenians pray,
"Rain, rain, dear Zeus,
Upon the fields and plains of Athens."

If you pray at all, keep your prayers as simple and inno-cent as this.

---

8. Everything happens for a positive purpose

Just as a doctor prescribes riding, cold baths, or walking barefoot, nature prescribes disease, injury, loss, or some form of disability. In the case of the doctor, prescriptions are meant to treat the patient. It is so with nature too. Nature orders certain events to further our destiny. We meet with these events like two blocks of stones in a wall meet with each other. They fit perfectly with each other to make the whole. This mutual integration is a universal principle. Countless bodies join together to make the world. Countless causes combine to make a single cause or destiny. Even common people generally understand this when they say, "It was brought upon him." Yes in-deed, it was prescribed for him.

Let's accept what comes our away like we accept a doctor's prescription. They may have a harsh flavour, but so does medicine that we swallow gladly hoping for bet-ter health. We should treat what nature prescribes us no differently than what a doctor prescribes us for our health. Even is what happens to you is unpleasant, accept it gladly. It is needed for the health and well-being of the universe – and even of Zeus himself. He would never let this happen to you unless it is for the benefit of the whole. It is not nature's way to bring anything upon you unless it is managed by her and it is beneficial to the world as a whole.

There are two reasons why you should accept whatever comes your way.

i.   It happens to you, has been prescribed for you, and concerns you. You are a strand in the tapestry created a long time ago as the oldest cause.

ii.   What happens to you is needed for the prosperity, success, and even survival of what directs the world. By breaking even a small part of the continuous fusion of causes and other elements, we damage the whole.

Every time you complain, you are doing your best to cause damage to the whole.

---

9. Don't give up when you fail

Don't be distressed, don't be despair and give up, if your practice falls short of principles. Return to your practice after each failure. Be thankful that, overall, you are behaving like a human, but have a genuine liking for your precepts. Philosophy is not a master, and you are not schoolboy. Philosophy is a remedy, like the sponge and egg white that are used to relieve sore eyes. It is not for public display but for private comfort.

All philosophy wants is what your nature wants. And you look for something that is different from what your nature wants.

"Yes, but what else is better?"

That's exactly how pleasure traps you. Isn't nobility better? Isn't openness, simplicity, kindness, piety? When you consider the precision, the smoothness with which our perception and reasoning happen, can there be anything better than the way we use our mind?

---

10. No one can force you to act against nature

Truth is hidden in obscurity. So, many philosophers say that we cannot know anything for certain. Even the Stoics admit that there are problems. Our conclusions can be challenged. Where is the person who doesn't fail? Think the same about material things. How impermanent, how worthless! Anyone can have them – a spendthrift, a whore, or a thief.

Look at your own associates. Even the best of them are difficult to put up with. And, for that matter, we can't even put up with ourselves.

In such darkness, in such a sewer, in all this unending flow of being and time, in changes imposed and changes endured, what can you prize highly? Or pursue seriously? No. What you need to do is to wait quietly for your natural end. Don't get impatient for it to come but be comforted by these two thoughts.

i.   Nothing can ever happen to us that is not natural.

ii.   It's within your power not to act against the divine spirit. No one can force you to do so.

---

11. Examine yourself in every step

What are you doing with your soul?

Examine yourself on this every step. What is in that part of your mind that controls everything? What kind of soul lives in you now? A child's? A teenager's? A woman's? A tyrant's? A dumb animal's? Or a wild animal's?

12. Goods of the mind versus material goods

What do ordinary people mean by "goods?"

Suppose you think it is things like discretion, self-control, justice, and courage. Then you wouldn't understand the quip "so many goods..." because it would mean nothing. But, if you thought of it in an unrefined way, then the quip would make sense to you. You'd have no trouble seeing its meaning.

Most of us see this difference. Otherwise, we wouldn't recognise the first meaning as jarring and reject it right away while accepting the second meaning, which refers to prestige and luxury as proper and clever.

Now for the test. Would you accept as goods and value them if it is of the type that fills your house and leaves no room even to ease yourself?

13. We never die, we are just transformed

I am made up of an element and a material. They did not come from nothing and so cannot become nothing. So, every part of me will one day be redesigned and transferred to another part of the universe. It will be transformed into something else, and that something into

STOIC MEDITATIONS • 67

something else. This process goes on repeating itself forever.

I was brought this way into the world, and so were my
parents and others before them.

This is so, even if the world is administered in finite
cycles.

---

14. Reason and reasoning are "directed"

Reason and reasoning are self-sufficient faculties. They
start on their own and are motivated by their own source
as they travel straight to their own goals. We call them
'directed' because they follow a course without deviating
from it.

---

15. What doesn't define you doesn't belong to you

The only things that belongs to humans are things that
define them. Nothing else can be demanded of us —nature does not promise them or is incomplete without
them. They are not our main goal. They are not even the
'good' that will help us reach the goal. If it properly be-
longed us, we could not disregard or reject them. We
would not think highly of those who do without them. If
these things were good, not having them would be in-
compatible with goodness. But, in reality, the more we
stay away or agree to stay away from such things, the
more we grow in goodness.

16. Thoughts determine the quality of mind

The quality of your mind is determined by the quality of its thoughts, and the soul is dyed by it. So colour it with thoughts like:

- *If it possible to live anywhere, it is possible to live the right way there.* Living anywhere is possible. Therefore, it is possible to live the right anywhere.

- *Things move towards their purpose, their final state.* Therefore, the final state of anything gives a clue as to its purpose and its good. A rational person's chief good is fellowship with others; it has been made clear long ago that this is the purpose of creation. This, of course, is obvious. Lower beings are made for higher beings, and higher beings are made for one another. Animate is superior to inanimate, and the rational is superior still.

17. It is insane to go after what is impossible

It is insane to go after what is impossible, yet the thoughtless person cannot stop doing it.

18. You can endure anything

Nothing can happen to you that you cannot endure. Your neighbours' experience is no different from yours. Yet they – either out of ignorance of what happened or out of a desire to show off – stand firm and undisturbed. For shame, ignorance and vanity should prove stronger than wisdom!

19. Things don't touch the soul

Outward things don't touch the soul. Not even just a bit. They don't have access to it, they have no power to move or direct it. It moves and directs itself, and judges things by its own standards.

20. What stands in the way is the way

People touch me deeply. My job is to do them good, and bear with them. But, when they try to prevent me from doing my proper work, they become indifferent to me – like the sun, the wind, or wild animals.

True, others may prevent us from doing certain things, but they cannot affect our will and our disposition. These will always safeguard and adapt themselves to changing conditions.

The mind can overcome and convert obstacles to its own main purpose. The obstacle to its work becomes its support. The barriers in the path become aids to its progress.

21. Honour the highest part of you

Honour that which is greatest in the universe, which is served by everything and governs everything. Honour the highest in yourself, the part that shares its nature with the greatest. Like everything else, you serve it and governed by it.

---

22. If your community is not harmed, neither are you

What does not harm the community does not harm the individual. When you imagine that you have been harmed, apply this rule: 'My community is not harmed, so neither am I." If your community is harmed, don't be angry at the culprit. Find out why his vision failed him.

---

23. All things pass – even your troubles

Think how quickly all things come into being and how quickly they pass away. The river of life flows without stopping. It is constantly changing, never standing still. There is the long stretch of infinity ahead of it and behind it. It is a vast abyss into which everything we see is lost. What sense does it make to fret and fume – as if your troubles are going to last forever?

---

24. You are a tiny part of the whole

- In the totality of everything, yours is a small share.
- In the totality of time, yours is a brief instant.
- In the totality of destiny, yours is a puny part.

25. What others do is their business

Has anyone done me wrong?

Let them take care of it. Their character and actions are theirs. What happened to me is a part of nature's plan. I will act according to my nature.

26. Pleasure and pain are what they are

Let no emotions of pleasure or pain effect your supreme part – your mind. Keep emotions confined to their place, away from it. If they enter your mind, don't try to resist them. Just use your reason. Don't think of them as good or bad.

27. Live with the gods

Live with the gods. How? By showing them that you accept whatever they give you and doing whatever they ask of you. You are a particle of the gods, which is your mind and your reason.

28. Don't be bothered by others' actions

Are you bothered by other people's smelly armpits and bad breath? How does it do you any good? With that armpit and with that mouth, that condition is bound to happen. They are endowed with reason, and if they took the time, they could easily understand what is offensive. Well and good, but you are also endowed with reason.

Use it to make the other person use theirs. Explain. Warn. If they pay attention, you cured them. No need for drama. Leave it to the street performers.

29. Live in accordance with nature

You can live on earth like you mean to live in the hereafter. If others won't let you, then quit the house of life, without losing anything. If there's smoke in the house, leave. What's the big deal about it?

As long as nothing like that happens to me, I stay. I am my own master, and no one can hinder me from doing what I choose. I choose to live in accordance with nature as a reasonable member of a social community.

30. The social fabric is created by the universe

The intentions of the universe are social. It created the lower forms to serve the higher. It then linked the higher forms to be dependent on each other. Observe how some are subordinates and others inter-connected. Each gets its due, and the best among them are aligned.

31. Think back on your life

How have you behaved in the past – to the gods, to your parents, to your siblings, spouse, children, teachers, tutors, friends, relatives, household? In all your dealings with them until now, can you fairly say that "Never a harsh word, never an injustice was delivered to a single person?"

Remember everything you have gone through and all that you have endured. The story of life is over, and you have done your assignment. Think of all the sights you have seen,

- How many pleasures and pains have you resisted?
- How many honours have you declined?
- How many times have you been considerate to the inconsiderate?

---

32. Reason orders the universe

"How is it that unskilled and untrained souls confuse the skilled and trained?"

"But what soul is skilled and trained?"

"The person who knows the beginning and the end. The person who knows how reason orders the universe and assigns everything a place and time, through the entire time.

33. Nothing outside of your body belongs to you. Soon you will be ashes or bones. Just a name, perhaps not even that – although a name is just an empty sound repeated again and again. The things we desire in life are vanity, corruption, and trash. We are like scuffling puppies or quarrelling children – all smiles one moment and in tears the next. Trust, decency, justice, and truth have fled to Olympus from this earth.

Why are you still here? Objects of the senses are shifting and unstable. Our senses are easily deceived. Our soul itself is mere vapour exhaled from blood[23] Fame in this world is worthless.

"What then?"

"Wait patiently for extinction and rebirth."

"What to do until that time comes?"

"Honour and bless the gods. Do good to people. Bear and forbear. Remember that nothing belongs to you outside the bounds of your poor body. They are not in your power.

---

33. Keep the straight road

Be steady as you go forward. Keep the straight road in your thinking and doing. Your will flows smoothly.

The soul of human beings and of the gods have two things in common:

i. It can never be affected by outside forces; and

ii. Its good comes from doing the right thing. Limit your desires to this.

---

34. If it is not of your doing, don't worry about it

If something is not of your doing, nor caused by you and the community is not affected by it, why worry about it? How can it harm society?

35. Even if the injury is imaginary, be kind

Don't be taken in by your first impressions. Help those in need as far as you can. They deserve it. But, if their hurt involves nothing morally significant, it is incorrect to think of them as injured. Be like the old man who eagerly begged for the orphan's toy, knowing well that it was all it was. [The old man knew that the toy is of little value. By begging for it, he made it look valuable. Similarly, we should know that the injury is not real, but we sympathise with the person anyway.]

"When you are on the platform crying for votes, have you forgotten how little worth they have?"

"Yes, but it is important to them."

"So, are you justified in sharing their stupidity?"

No matter how many setbacks I had, I was always fortunate. Who is fortunate? The person who gives himself the gifts of fortune: good character, good intentions, and good actions.

BOOK 6

Play Your Role in the World

1. Reason knows no malice

Nature is flexible and obedient. Reason, which controls nature, has no motive to do evil. It has no malice, it doesn't injure anyone, and nothing is harmed by it. Everything is born and fulfilled by its orders.

2. Always do what needs doing

Do the right thing. Never mind whether you are freezing or warm, heavy-eyed or fully rested, despised or honoured, or about to die. (Death is a part of life. Even when we die, nothing more is asked of us than doing that moment's work.)

3. Look below the surface

Look below the surface. Don't let a thing's true nature or value escape you.

4. All material things change quickly

All material things change quickly. They are either transformed and united with the universe or dispersed into fragments.

5. Reason knows its purpose and conditions

Reason, the controller, fully knows the conditions, the purpose, and the materials of its work.

6. Not imitating is the best revenge

Not to be like that is the best revenge

7. Take delight in serving others

Let this be your delight and refreshment. Move from one service to the community to another, keeping the gods in mind.

8. Reason is roused and directed by itself

Our reasoning faculty is roused and directed by itself. It makes of itself what it chooses. It imposes the choice on its experiences.

9. There is only one universal nature

One universal nature brings about everything. There is no rival to it. There is nothing beyond it and nothing within it. There is nothing apart from it.

10. Does the universe have a purpose?

Either the universe is a jumble of things randomly coming together and breaking apart, or it has unity, order, and design. If random, why would we want to live in disorder and chaos? Why would we care about anything except dying? Why bother to think about anything at all since they all will break apart sooner or later anyway? But, if the opposite is true, then I respect, I stand firmly, I put my trust in the divine.

11. When upset, get back to harmony quickly

When things upset you, gain control over them quickly. Don't be upset for longer than you can help. If you make it a habit of getting back to harmony, you will become a master at it.

12. Turn to philosophy often

If you had a mother and a step-mother, you would do what is your duty to the step-mother while turning to your mother continually. So, it is here: the court life and philosophy. Continually return to philosophy to renew yourself. Your court life – and you in it – will seem bearable.

---

13. Look beneath the surface

When meat and other delicacies are in front of you, think:

- This is dead fish, foul, or pig; or
- This vintage is grape juice; or
- My purple robe is sheep's wool stained with shellfish blood; or
- Making love is a friction of the members and ejaculation.

Reflections like these go to the bottom of things. They pierce through them, exposing what they really are.

You should apply the same process to life as well. When things appear trustworthy, lay them bare. Observe how trivial they are. Strip away the attractive description that dignifies them.

Pretentiousness is an arch deceiver. It deludes you when you believe that your work has great merit.

[Here, Marcus Aurelius has a reference to Crates and Xenocrates, the meaning of which is not clear.]

---

14. The universal mind is social

Ordinary people admire physical things, such things made of wood or stones or things such as figs, vines, or olives. People with more advanced minds admire things that move, such as flocks of birds and herds of animals.

People whose minds are even more advanced admire the rational mind – not the universal mind, but the one that is skilful in some art or craft or even the one that controls others.

But, people who value a rational, social, and universal mind aren't interested other things. All they are concerned about is their own minds – how to be rational and social, how to work with others for this purpose.

---

15. Don't get attached to ever-fleeting things

Some things come into being quickly while others go out of it just as quickly. Even as a thing comes into being, some part of it is already gone. Change and fluidity constantly remake the world, just as the relentless flow of time remakes eternity.

In this running river, where can you find a firm foothold? What can you find of value among the many things that are rapidly passing by you? It is like attachment to a sparrow that is flying by you. The moment you do it, the bird is gone.

Your life is just an inhalation from the air and an exhalation from the blood. There is no difference between breathing a single breath (as we do every moment) and having the ability to breathe for a long time (as we have done since our birth) only to give it back someday to the source.

16. Understand your purpose

What is it that we should value in ourselves?

- Not transpiration. We share it with plants.
- Not respiration. We share it with animals, domestic and wild.
- Not perception of the senses, the pulls of impulse, the social instinct, or eating and relieving yourself afterwards.

Then what?

The clapping of hands? No, not the clapping of tongues either – that's what cheap praise is. Throw out public recognition.

What is left that's of value?

In my judgement, this: To understand what we are designed for. That is the goal of all trades and crafts. Every trade aims to adapt a product to the purpose for which it was produced: the farmer takes care of the vine, the trainer the horse, the breeder the dogs. This is the value we are looking for. Once you understand this, nothing else will tempt you.

Give up all other ambitions you now value. Otherwise, you won't be your own master. You won't be independent of others. You won't be able to resist passion. You will always be envious and jealous, afraid that others might rob you of those things. You will plot against those who have those things so you can get them for yourself. If you believe you must have them, you will have internal conflict. You may even end up blaming the gods.

STOIC MEDITATIONS • 83

On the other hand, if you respect and value your own understanding, it will leave you satisfied with yourself, at one with humankind, and in harmony with the divine. So embrace what the gods hand you or will you to do.

17. Virtue moves steadily forward

The elements move in all directions – above, below, and around us. But, virtue doesn't move at random. She is more divine, moves serenely forward, and in ways we cannot understand.

18. People behave in irrational ways

People behave in strange ways. They won't praise their colleagues who live among them, yet crave for themselves the praise of future generations they have never seen and will never see. They might as well be upset because their ancestors didn't praise them.

19. What is hard is not impossible

Don't assume that something is impossible because you find it hard. Recognize that if something is possible and proper for a human being to do, you can do it too.

20. Be cautious without being suspicious

In a ring, an opponent can injure us with his nails or bruise our head by colliding with it. We aren't offended, and we don't protest. We don't attribute malicious intent to him. However, we become cautious towards him and keep a friendly distance, even though we are not antagonistic or suspicious.

Do the same thing in other areas of your life too. Let's overlook many things in our fellow human beings, but keep our distance, without suspicion or ill will.

---

21. Self-delusion and ignorance are harmful

If you can show me and prove to me that I am wrong in my thinking or in my actions, I will gladly change. I am only after the truth. Truth doesn't harm anyone. Persistent self-delusion and ignorance do.

---

22. Do your duty and don't be distracted

I do my duty. I am not interested in the rest. They are inanimate or irrational, or someone who doesn't know the way and are misled.

---

23. Be generous and liberal with irrational animals

Be generous and liberal with irrational animals, with material things. You can reason and they can't. Treat them with fellowship. In all things, call upon the gods for help. Don't worry about the length of time. Just half-a-day should be sufficient.

24.   In death, we are all the same

In death, Alexander the Great was no different from a stable boy. Both were absorbed by the universe the same way and dissolved into atoms.

25. The universe is vast

Think how many things are going on in your (as well as other people's) mind and body each and every moment. Then why should it be a surprise to you that an infinitely greater number of things – in fact, everything that arises in this vast universe – exist, all at the same time?

26. Complete your tasks methodically

If someone asked you to spell your name, would you shout out each letter loudly? If you did that and others got upset, would you be upset in turn? Wouldn't you rather spell the letters quietly to yourself? Likewise, your duty is made of several parts. Pay attention to each one, but don't make a fuss or return anger for anger. Complete your task methodically.

27. Don't be angry at others

It is uncivilised to stop people from doing what they believe to be in their proper concerns and interests. Yet, this is what you are doing when you get angry if they misbehave. After all, they were only following their concerns and interests. You say they are mistaken? Then tell them and explain it to them, instead of being angry.

---

28. Death ends everything

Death is the end of sense perception, the end of being controlled by your passions, the end of mental activity, and the end of serving our body.

---

29. Life marches on while the soul pauses

Shame on the soul for pausing on the road of life while the body still marches ahead.

---

30. Don't let power carry you away

Be careful not to become imperious with royal purple – this can happen. Keep yourself simple, good, pure, reverent, unassuming, and devoted to your duty. Try your best to be the person that philosophy tried to make you. Revere the gods, look after your fellow-humans. Life is short. The only reward here is our character within and unselfish action without.

Model yourself after Antoninus. Remember how he always insisted on actions based on reason. His calm expression and his character. His serenity and his sweetness. His modesty. His zeal to investigate things fully, never dismissing anything until he understood it fully. His willingness to put up with criticism without returning it. His lack of hurry and his avoidance of informers.

His shrewd judgment of character and actions. His avoidance of nervousness, suspicion, or empty rhetoric. His contentment with the basics – house, bed, dress, meals, and service. His industriousness and his patience. His frugal diet, which helped him to be at work from morning till night, even foregoing calls of nature. His reliability and constancy of friendship. His tolerance of those who openly questioned him, welcoming modifications to his ideas with respect. His piety without a trace of superstition. Remember all this, so when your time comes, your conscience will be as clear as his.

31. Awake from your sleep

Return to yourself. Remember who you truly are. Awake from your sleep. Realize it is all dreams that troubled you. Being clear-headed now, look at what meets your wakeful eye.

32. Only the present matters

I am made of a body and a mind. To the body, everything is indifferent. It cannot make distinctions. To the mind, the only things that are not indifferent are its own activities because these are under its control. Even with them, only the present matters. Things that lie in the past or the future are indifferent.

33. Stress is natural

Pain of hand or foot is natural when they are doing their own job. Likewise, it is natural for human beings to feel stress, if they are doing the work of a human being. How can it be a bad thing if it is in accordance with nature?

34.   Perverse pleasures

What kind of perverse pleasures do robbers, murderers of relatives, and tyrants enjoy?

35. Stand by Your Conviction

Have you noticed how professionals accommodate the demands of their unskilled employer up to a point, and yet stand by the rules of their profession and refuse to bend them? Isn't it shocking that a builder or a physician should have more respect for their profession than a human being has for theirs, even though they share it with the gods?

36.   Everything comes from the same source

In the universe,
- Asia and Europe are two small corners,
- Oceans are a drop,
- Mount Athos is a puny lump of earth, and
- The vastness of time is a pin's point in eternity.

Everything is petty, temporary, and perishable. Everything springs, directly or indirectly, from one source: Reason, universal and supreme. Even the lion's open jaws, the deadly poison, the bramble bush, and the quagmire are all by-products of something noble and beautiful. They are not alien to what you revere. Remember, everything comes from the same source.

37. The present includes everything

If you have seen the present, you have seen everything since the beginning of time until the end of the world. All things are one kind. All things are one form.

38. A bond unites everything

Think of the bond that unites everything in the universe. They are all dependent on one another. All are interconnected and in sympathy with one another. Their orderly procession is brought about by the pull and push of tension and the unity of everything.

39. Adapt to where you are

Adapt yourself to the environment assigned to you. Love your fellow human beings with whom your destiny is bound.

40.   The way of the universe

Tools, instruments, and utensils work when they do what they are designed for, even if the person who made them is not around. But, with things designed by nature, the power that created them is always with them. All the more reason why you should revere it. Be confident that only if you act according to its will, you will have all things to your liking. This is the way of the universe too.

41. Nothing outside of you is good or bad

If you think that something over which you have no control can be good or bad, then if what you define as 'bad' happens to you, you will blame the gods and be bitter against people you think are responsible for it. We do many unjust things by this kind of thinking. But, if you limit your idea of good and bad to only your actions, you will neither blame the gods nor treat others as your enemies.

42.   We all work toward the same goal

All of us are working together towards the same goal. Some do so consciously with understanding and others without even knowing it. (Heraclitus put it this way, I believe: "Even in their sleep people are at work," thus contributing their share to the universal end.) Some fall short in one task, others in another. Even those who complain, obstruct, and undo things help as much as anyone.

So, it is for you to decide who you want to work with. The force that directs everything will make of you all the same and give you a place among helpers and fellow-workers. Just make sure that it is not, as Chrysippus would say, a clown's part put there for laughs.

43. Do your assigned work

Does the sun try to do the rain's work? Or Asclepius Demeter's? How about the stars? Aren't they all different and yet work together towards the same goal?

44. What is good for the universe is good for you

If the gods have made decisions about me and what should happen to me, then they are good decisions. It is hard to think of the gods making poor decisions. What would be their motive to do so? What do they gain? What would the universe, which they look after, gain? Even if they don't care for me, they care for the universe. Therefore, I should look at anything that happens kindly.

Suppose they took no thought at all about anything (an impious thought), then let's stop sacrifice, prayer, vow, and all other actions, believing that the gods are right there with us. Even so, I can take care of myself, look after my interests, as well as the interests of those who live in accordance with nature.

My own nature is rational and civic. I have a city and a country. Like Marcus, I have Rome. As a human being, I have the universe. Therefore, what is good for those communities is the sole good for me.

45.   What is good for the universe is also good for fellow human beings

Whatever happens to an individual is for the good of the universe. That itself is good enough. But, if you look closely, you will also see that, as a general rule, what is good for one person is also good for their fellow human beings. ('Good' as ordinarily understood.)

46.   You've all seen them before

The performances in places of entertainment tire you after a while. They are monotonous, and you have seen them all before. So it is with life. Its ups and downs of life, causes and effects – everything the same.

How much longer?

47. Be truthful and fair

Keep in mind that people of every profession, of every nation, all the way down to Philistion, Phoebus, and Origanion have died. Think about the host of others. Where they have all gone, we have to go there too.

- Heraclitus, Pythagoras, and Socrates, the revered sages;

- Heroes of the past, the captains and the kings who came afterwards;
- Eudoxus, Hipparchus, Archimedes, and others;
- The smart, the sublime, the untiring, the resourceful the resolute; and
- Even those who made fun of this brief, fragile life such as Menippus and associates.

Think about them often. All dead for a long time. How are they any worse now? What about others, whose name we don't even know?

There is only one thing that is precious in this life: to live one's life truthfully and fairly, and be charitable even with those who are untruthful and unfair.

48. Become aware of other people's virtues

If you want to uplift your spirit, think of the qualities of your friends. You may find one person modest, another unassuming, yet another generous and so on. Nothing is a greater remedy for depression than seeing examples of virtues in the people around us. They are all around us. Keep this in mind.

49. Accept the time allotted to you

Do you worry that you weigh what you weigh, and not 300 pounds? So why bother about living so many years only and not more? You accept what and how much is given to you in terms of other areas. Do the same with the length of your life.

50. Attempt to convince others if you can

Try your best to convince others. If someone totally obstructs you, go along with them, but use the obstacle to practice some other virtue. You cannot expect do the impossible.

"Then what do I do?"

"You attempted. In that, you succeeded. And that is the objective of living."

51. Your good is in your actions

If you are ambitious, you will try to find your good in others. If you are self-indulgent, you will try to find your good in your senses. If you are a person of understanding, you will try to find your good in your own actions.

52. It's your opinion that upsets you

You don't have to have an opinion about anything. Nothing needs to upset you. Things have no power to force you to have an opinion about them.

53.Pay attention to what people say

Pay careful attention to what people say. Try your best to understand where they are coming from.

54. What is not good for the community is not good for you

What is not good for the beehive is not good for the bee.

55. Don't vilify authorities

If the crew belittle the captain or patients their doctor, then whose authority would they accept? And, how would this other person ensure the safety of the crew or the health of the patients?

56. Life is fleeting and not predictable

How many came into this world with me! How many of them have already left!

57. A sick mind is like a sick body

To a person with jaundice, honey tastes bitter. To a person bitten by a mad dog, water looks terrifying. To a child, a ball is a great treasure.

Why should I be angry with anyone, then?

Isn't a person whose thinking is erroneous similar to a person with jaundice or hydrophobia?

58.   No one can stop you

No one can stop you from living according to the laws of your personal nature. Nothing can happen to you against the laws of universal nature.

59.   Remember, time erases everything

People try to please miserable folks. They pursue miserable ends in miserable ways. How quickly time covers everything! How many has it covered already!

BOOK 7

Nature is Logical

1. Everything is commonplace and fleeting

What is evil? The same thing you have seen before. Remind yourself that you have seen this many times, like you have seen many other things. Everywhere – above and below – you will find nothing but the same old thing. It fills all history books – modern, ancient, and current. It fills our homes, our cities. Nothing is new. Everything is familiar and short-lived.

2. A new life is within your reach

How can your principles die, unless the thoughts behind them are forgotten? It is in your power to fan the flames of these thoughts. You can form the right opinion about anything. Given this ability, why should you be disturbed? (If it is beyond your understanding, it is of no concern to you.) Understand this and stand tall. A new life is within your reach. Look at things the way you did once. Life begins again.

---

3. The measure of your worth

A pointless pageant, a stage play, flocks of sheep, herds of cattle, military exercises, a bone thrown among dogs, a breadcrumb thrown into a fishpond, the labours of ants, the running of frightened mice – that is life. In the middle of it all, you should take a stand: be good-tempered, be without contempt, and yet be aware that your worth is measured by what you devote your energy to.

---

4. Attend to what is said and what is meant

In a discussion, focus on what is being said. When action is needed, focus on what is being done. Know what is said and what is meant.

---

5. Act for the good of everyone

Have I understood this right? If I have, I will apply it as a tool given to me by nature. If I haven't, I will turn it over to someone else who can do it better, unless I have a reason not to. Otherwise, I will enlist the assistance of a helper who, with the help of my ruling faculty, can do what is timely and needed for the community. For everything I do – either by myself or with someone else – should have only one purpose: doing what is useful and well-suited to all.

6. Fame is short-lived

How many who were famous are forgotten! How many who celebrated the famous are long gone!

7. Don't be ashamed to ask for help

Don't be ashamed to ask for help. You should do your duty like a soldier. How could you do it if you are lame (hurt) and unable to climb out of a hole yourself, except with the help of a comrade?

8. Don't let the future worry you

Don't let the future worry you. You will meet it – if you have to – with reason, the resource you now use to deal with life.

9. All things are interconnected

All things are interconnected. A sacred bond unites them. There is hardly anything that stands on its own. Everything is harmonious. Everything works together to form this one universe. This one universe is made up of all things. There is one God, who is in all things. All being is one. All law (common reason shared by all intelligent beings) is one. All truth is one, if indeed there is only one path to perfection for beings that are alike in kind and reason.

10. Everything goes back to it source

Soon, every material thing disappears into the universal nature. Soon, everything that makes other things happen is taken back to the universal reason. Soon, the memory of everything is buried in eternity.

11. Nature implies reason

For a rational person, what is according to nature is according to reason.

12. Stand erect. Don't be made to stand direct

Stand erect. Don't be made to stand direct[24].

13. We are made to function together as one

Rational beings are made to function together as one, just as limbs in a body function together as one. Both are made similarly for mutual cooperation. You will understand this better if you tell yourself that you are a limb of a larger, rational body. If you think of it just an [unconnected] limb, then you don't love people from your heart. You find no joy in being kind for its own sake. You are being kind because it is the proper thing to do, not realising that you are doing good to yourself.

STOIC MEDITATIONS • 101

14. External happenings are not evil

If something happens, the parts of me that are affected may complain, if they like. But, if I don't interpret it as bad or evil, I am not harmed. No one compels me to do so.

15. Be an emerald and keep your colour

No matter what others say or do, it is my job to be good. Like gold, emerald, or purple may say to itself, "No matter what others say or do, it is my job to be an emerald and keep my colour."

16. We make our own fear and pain

The mind doesn't disturb itself. It doesn't scare itself or cause itself pain. If others can frighten it or cause it pain, so be it. But, it is never scared or pained by its own assumptions. Let the body do whatever it can to avoid hurt. If it is hurt, let it complain. But, the soul – the part that feels and judges fear and pain – suffers nothing. You cannot force it to do otherwise. The mind is self-sufficient. It doesn't have any needs, except those of its own making. Neither can it be disturbed, unless it is of its own making.

17. Don't let imagination rule your mind

Eudemonia (happiness) means a 'good god within' or 'reason within.' So, Imagination, what are you doing here? Get back to where you came from. I don't need you. I know it is my habit that brought you here, so I have nothing against you. Just go away.

18. Change is the way of nature

Afraid of change? What can exist without change? What is more pleasing or more suitable to nature? Could you take a hot bath unless the firewood has undergone a change? Could you be nourished if food hasn't undergone a change? Could you achieve anything useful without change? Don't you see? It is just the same with you, and as necessary to nature.

19. Time swallows everything up

All bodies are carried through life as though through a rushing stream. By their nature, they unite and co-operate with the whole, just as our body parts do with one another. How many a Socrates, a Chrysippus, an Epictetus has time already swallowed up? Remember this when you deal with any person or thing.

20. Do the right thing, the right way, at the right time

Only one thing troubles me: The fear that I may do the wrong thing against nature, in the wrong way, or at the wrong time.

21. Soon, everything will be forgotten

Soon, you will have forgotten the world. Soon, the world will have forgotten you.

22. Love even those who make mistakes

It is uniquely human to love even those who make mistakes and go wrong. This happens if when they do wrong, you realise that they are related to you. Their ignorance is not intentional. In a short while, neither of you will be alive. Most importantly, you are not harmed. They haven't weakened your master faculty, Reason.

23. Nature creates and transforms

Nature takes the universal substance (as if it were wax) and moulds it into a horse. Then it melts the horse and makes it into a tree, then a human being, and then some other thing. Each exists for only a short time. It does the container no harm to be put together or broken apart.

24.   Anger is unnatural

An angry look is unnatural. It is completely against nature. If you are angry often, your beauty is destroyed. After a while, it is completely gone, and you cannot regain it. From this, understand that being angry is contrary to reason. If we lose the ability to see our mistakes, what's the point in living?

25. Change keeps the world young

Nature, which controls everything, will soon change all that you see and use it as material for something else. It will do so over and over again, so the world is always new.

26. Try to understand others

When someone offends you, ask yourself what good or ill they thought would come out of it. If you understand that, you will not be puzzled or angry but will sympathise with them.

- Your ideas may not be better than, or close to, theirs. If this is so, you have to excuse them.
- But, if you have gone beyond their thinking and have different ideas of good and ill, then they are mistaken and so deserve to be treated with compassion.

27. Appreciate the things you have now

Don't dream about things you don't have. Instead, think about the best things you now have and how much you would crave them if you didn't have them. At the same time, don't value them so much that you will be upset if you lose them.

28. Do what is just and rest in yourself

Rest in yourself. The rational principle that rules us has this quality: it is content with itself when it does what is just and thus achieves peace.

29. Let other people's mistakes rest with them

Do away with vain imagination. Don't be a puppet of passion. Limit yourself to the present. Understand well what happens to you and to others. Analyze everything to understand what is cause and what is material. Meditate upon your last hour. Let other people's mistakes rest with them.

30.　Focus your mind on what is happening

Direct your attention to what is said. Focus your mind on what happens and what makes it happen.

31. Law rules all

Beautify yourself with simplicity and modesty. Be indifferent to things that lie between virtue and vice. Love humankind. Follow God. The sage says, "Law rules all," and it is enough to remember this.

32. Death is either dispersion or change

Death. If it is atoms, they are extinguished or dispersed. If it is unity, it is transmuted (changed).

33. Pain is endurable

Pain. Unbearable pain carries us off. Chronic pain is always endurable. The mind is untouched by the body and remains calm. The ruling faculty is unaffected.

34.   Fame is short-lived

Fame. Take a look at the mind (of those who seek fame). Look at what they are, what they avoid, and what they go after. Think. How speedily the things of today are buried under those of tomorrow – just as one layer of drifting sand is quickly covered by another.

35. Death is not frightening

"If you have the greatness of mind to grasp all time and all reality, do you think our human life will mean much to you?"

"No, how could it?"

"Then, you won't think that death is very frightening?"

"No, certainly not."[25]

36. Being good with a bad reputation

It is royal to do good and be abused.[26]

37. The mind doesn't regulate itself

The mind orders the face on how it should look. It is a shame that the mind doesn't order to regulate itself.

38. Events don't care for you

Don't be upset at the world. It doesn't care.[27]

39. Bring joy to humans and to the gods

Bring joy to the immortal gods and to us.

40.   The cycle of life
The lives of human beings are reaped like ears of corn.
One is born, another dies.[28]

41. There is a reason for everything
If the gods don't care for my two children, there must be
a good reason even for this.[29]

42. What is just and good is on my side
What is just and good is on my side.[30]

43. Don't be carried by the emotions of others
No joining others in their crying. No quickening of the
pulse.

44. How you act is what matters
Then the only proper response I can make is this: You
are mistaken, my friend, if you think that any person
worth his salt should spend his time caring about the dangers of dying and living. You have to consider only one
thing in performing any action. Are you acting rightly or
wrongly, as a good person or like a bad one[31].

45. Stand your ground

In truth, it is like this, gentlemen. When you have taken up your stand, either you think it is best for you, or someone in authority asked you to. There, I believe, is where you should stand and face the danger. Don't worry about danger or about anything else before duty.[32]

46. Don't worry about your lifespan

My good friend, consider this. Is noble and good different from keeping yourself and your friends free from danger? Instead of clinging to life at all costs, shouldn't a true human being dismiss the thought of death and longevity from their mind?

Let them leave that to the will of the gods and accept what women say, 'No one can escape destiny' and turn their attention to the next problem: how best to live the life given to them.

47. Look at the bigger picture

Look at the circling stars, as if they revolved around you. Often think of the dance of the elements changing and changing again. Thoughts like these will wash off the dirt of life on earth.

48. See the harmony in diversity

Plato said this well. If you want to talk to people, you need to look down on the earth as though from a high watchtower. Assemblies, armies, farms. Mating and parting, birth and death. Noisy courtrooms, and deserted places. Foreign people of every kind feasting, bargaining and mourning. Observe this diverse crowd. See the harmonious order in this diversity.

49. The rhythm of life doesn't change

Look back over the past. Empires rose and fell. From this, you can foresee the future. It will have the same pattern, down to the last detail. Creation marches on, and you cannot break step with it. To observe the lives of people for forty years is the same as observing them for forty thousand years. What more will you see?

50. Everything returns to their source

All that is born of earth should return to earth, all that is born of heaven should return to heaven.[33] The atoms are pulled apart. The elements – which really don't care – disperse.

51. Face whatever happens

With food and drinks and magic spells
Seeking a novel way to frustrate death

To labour cheerfully and so endure
The wind that blows from heaven.[34]

52. Better professional versus better human

Better wrestler, yes. But, a better citizen? Modest? Disciplined? Resourceful? Forgiving of others' faults?

53. Reasonable actions will not harm you

There is nothing to fear if you do things that are in line with reason (which both humans and the gods share). If our effort that is in line with reason is profitable, no harm will come to us.

54. You have this power all the time

Everywhere and in every moment, you have the power to
- accept what happens with humility,
- treat your associates justly, and
- examine every impression of the day, so nothing irrational enters our mind.

55. Do what is according to nature

Don't look around to understand what directs other people's behaviour. Look straight ahead to where nature is taking you – both universal nature (what is happening to you) and your own nature (what you do).

Human beings should do what is according their nature. All other things are constituted for the use of rational beings. By this law, lower order things exist for the good of higher order things. Higher beings are designed for the good of each other.

- The most important thing is to do our duty.
- The second thing is to resist bodily urges. Our ruling faculty is designed to put up a fence around them and not be overcome by animal-like impulses and sensations. With good reason. The reasoning faculty is designed to be their master.
- The third thing is to avoid credulity and deception.

The mind that understands this will go straight ahead and hold its own.

56. Don't look back on the past

Think of yourself as dead. Your life story is over. Now, live the rest of your life according to nature.

57. Love only what happens to you

Love only what happens to you. It is destined to happen. What is better than this?

58. Use your experiences to your benefit

In everything that happens, keep this before your eyes. The same thing happened to other people. They resented it, were surprised by it, and complained about it. Where are they now? Nowhere.

Then why do you want to follow their example? These anxieties are foreign to nature. Why not leave it to those who cause them and are alarmed by them? Why don't you concentrate on the right way to use your experiences? You can use them well because they are your raw material to work on. Pay attention only to yourself. Resolve to be a good person in everything you do.

59. The fountain of good within you

Dig deep within. There is a fountain of good there. Keep digging, and it will bubble up.

60. Keep your body stable

Your body should be stable, without irregularities in movement or in rest. The mind shows its intelligence and decency through facial expressions. That's what the whole body needs as well. Observe all these things without special effort.

61. Living is like wrestling

The art of life is more like wrestling than dancing. It demands that you stand ready and firm to face sudden and unexpected attacks.

62. You don't need approval

Look at the people whose approval you seek and understand what their ruling principles are. If you do that, you won't blame them for their misjudgments. Nor will you seek their approval based on their principles.

63. People's behaviour is not intentional

They say that no one intentionally wants to cut off their soul from truth. The same holds true for justice, self-control, kindliness, or any other virtue. Keep this in mind constantly, and you will deal with people more gently.

64. Pain is temporary and bearable

When you are in pain, immediately remind yourself of this. There is no disgrace in pain. It does not damage your mind, which suffers no harm either to its rational or social part. In most cases, the saying of Epictetus that pain is neither unbearable nor unending should help, as long as you remember its limits and don't exaggerate them in your imagination.

And, always keep this in mind too: We may not realise this, but many things you find uncomfortable – such as drowsiness, fever, loss of appetite – are of the same nature as pain. When you are bothered by any of these, tell yourself that you are giving into pain.

65. Don't reciprocate inhuman feelings

When people act in inhuman ways, make sure you don't feel the same way towards them as they do towards others.

66. The quality of your soul decides who you really are

How do we know that Telauges wasn't a better man than Socrates?

It is all very well to argue that Socrates died a nobler death, debated with the Sophists better, and showed better physical endurance on cold nights; and, when he was ordered to arrest Leon of Salamis,[35] he preferred to refuse or that he walked the streets with a swagger (although the truth of this last may be questioned).

But, the real questions are these:

- What kind of soul did he have?
- Did he ask for anything more than to treat others with justice and the gods with reverence?
- Was he annoyed at other peoples' faults?
- Did he make himself a slave of other people's ignorance?

- Did he accept whatever naturally happened to him and not go looking for something unnatural? Or put up with it as something unbearable?
- Did he allow his mind to be influenced by bodily experiences?

---

67. The mind has the power to control its domain

Nature has not blended your body and mind so inseparably that your mind cannot establish its own boundaries and control its domain.

- It is perfectly possible to be godlike without anyone realising it. Remember this.
- You need very few things to be happy.
- You don't have to give up your hopes of achieving freedom, self-respect, unselfishness, and obeying God, just because you are not an expert on dialectics or physics.

---

68. Live your days in peace

Live your days in untroubled serenity. Refuse to be forced even though the world may scream at you with its demands, even though the wild beasts may tear your body to bits. In all this, there is nothing that can stop your mind from being serene, from correctly understanding what is happening, and from making use of your experience. And, to let your judgment say to your impression, "This is what you really are, regardless of your appearance," and consider it an opportunity to say, "You are what I have been looking for."

The present moment is always an opportunity for exercising reason and fraternity, things that are common to both humans and the gods. Both believe that there is nothing that is hard to deal with and they have seen it all before.

69. Live each day as your last

To live each day as your last – never in a frenzy, never indifferent, never pretentious – is the perfection of character.

70. The gods are patient. You should be too

The gods live eternally, yet they don't resent having to put up with human beings and their behaviour throughout eternity. Not only that, they even show every possible care and concern for humans. You live here for a moment. Are you going to lose patience with them, even though you are a wrongdoer yourself?

71. Try to escape your faults, not others'

How ridiculous that you don't try to flee from your faults (which is possible), but try to flee from other people's faults (which is not possible)!

72. What is inferior?

If our reasoning and social faculty finds something as un-intelligent and unsocial, then it correctly judges it as inferior.

73. Don't look for applause

You have done a good action, and someone benefited from it. Why are you, like an idiot, holding out for more – such as applause for your kindness, or some favour in return?

74. You receive benefits by giving them

No one tires of receiving benefits, but benefits come from acting in accordance with nature. So never tire of receiving such benefits by doing beneficial acts for others.

75. Whatever happens is rational

Nature had the impulse to create an orderly world. It follows then that everything that happens now is logical. If this is not so, then it would follow that the world was created for an irrational purpose. Remember this, and you will face many things more calmly.

BOOK 8

Take Refuge in Your Inner Citadel

1. Principles to follow

You will less likely be self-satisfied if you remember this: You cannot claim to have lived like a philosopher all your life, not even all your adult life. It is obvious to you as well as to others that it is still beyond you. Your mind is disorderly, and it has not become any easier to be a philosopher. Your life plan is also against it.

Once you clearly understand all this, forget how you look to others. Be content to live the rest of your life as decided by nature. Learn to understand her will and let nothing distract you. You have not been successful so far in finding the good life. You cannot find it in logic, wealth, fame, worldly pleasures, or anything else.

"Where can you find the secret?"

"In doing what your nature requires."

"How?"

"By closely following the principles that regulate your impulses and actions."

"What principles?"

"Principles that tell us what is good and bad for us. For example, nothing is good unless it helps you to become just, self-disciplined, courageous, and independent. Nothing is bad, except what does the opposite."

---

2. Let your actions be right

For every action ask:

- How will it affect me?
- Will I regret it?

Soon you will be dead and forgotten. Meanwhile, if what you do is fit for a rational and social being, why worry about anything else?

---

3. Kings don't compare to philosophers

What are Alexander, Caesar, and Pompey compared to Diogenes, Heraclitus, and Socrates? The philosophers looked at things, their causes, what they are made of, and how they were guided by the same ruling principle. But, as to the others, how many things they had to take care of! To how many things were they slaves!

---

4. Don't expect people to change

You may break your heart, but people will continue to do what they do.

5. Be untroubled and follow nature

The first rule: Be untroubled. Nature controls everything, and soon you will vanish into nothingness, like Hadrian and Augustus.

The second rule: Fix your eyes on what you have to do. Remember, you must be a good human being. Do what nature demands of you without hesitation. Speak what is just as you see it, but do so with courtesy, modesty, and sincerity.

6. Change is not fearful

Nature's task is to shift things everywhere, to move things from here to there, and transform them into this to that. Everywhere there is change, yet we need to fear nothing. All things – including the way they are arranged – are familiar to us.

7. What nature demands of us

Every nature thrives when it goes on its way very well. A rational nature goes well when

- there is no acceptance of misleading or false impressions;
- there is no impulse towards unsocial actions;
- all desires and rejections are confined to what lies within its power; and
- there is welcome acceptance of whatever nature demands of us.

What nature demands of us is truly a part of her as a leaf's nature is a part of a plant's. The difference is that the nature shared by the leaf has no feelings or reason and can be frustrated; the nature shared by a human being cannot be frustrated and is intelligent and just. It assigns to all human beings equally their fair share of time, being, purpose, activity, and experiences. Look closely. You will see such equality is not identical in every aspect, but is in totality.

8. You have time

You don't have time for reading, but you have time to curb your arrogance. You have time to rise above pleasures and pains. You have time to resist the lure of fame. You have time not to be annoyed with the foolish and ungrateful. And, yes, even to care for them.

9. Don't complain about court life

Don't let anyone – not even you – overhear you complaining about court life again.

10. Pleasure is neither good nor beneficial

Remorse is reproaching yourself for losing something that's to your benefit. Now, what is good is always beneficial and must concern every human being, but if it's an opportunity for pleasure, no good person would ever

regret losing it. It follows, therefore, that pleasure is neither good nor beneficial.

11. Think about the nature of things

What is this thing in itself? What is its substance? What
is its form, its matter? Why is it in this world? How long
will it be around?

12. Following nature is a more suitable thing

When you resist waking up in the morning, remind yourself of this: Going about doing the duties you owe society
is following nature's laws as well as your own. Sleeping
is something we share with other animals. To follow your
own nature is the more appropriate, more suitable, and,
indeed, the most agreeable thing to do.

13. Examine every impression

If possible, make it a habit to examine the essential nature of every impression – how it affects the self, its ethics, and its logic.

14. People's actions are based on their beliefs

Whenever you meet with someone, ask yourself this
question: What do good and bad mean to this person? If
this is what they believe about pleasure and pain and
their causes, about fame and disgrace, about life and

death, why should you be surprised or shocked by what they do? It is consistent with their beliefs. They have no choice.

15. Don't be surprised by the way things are

No one is surprised when a fig tree produces figs. Similarly, we should be ashamed of our surprise when the world acts the way it does. It would embarrass a doctor to act surprised when a patient has a fever, and a ship's captain wouldn't be surprised by a headwind.

16. Changing your mind is a free act

When you change your mind and follow the person who corrects your error, you are not giving up your independence. You are doing so voluntarily, based on your will, your judgment, and your thinking.

17. It's pointless to blame others

If it is your choice, why do it? If it is someone else's, who do you blame? The gods? Atoms? Both are foolish. No one is to blame. If you can, correct the person who is responsible. If you cannot, repair the damage. If you can do neither, why blame others? It is pointless.

18. Things don't vanish, they transform

What dies doesn't disappear. It continues to be in this world, changing, broken into different particles – the elements that form the universe and yourself. They, in turn, change again without complaining.

19. We are created to do our work

Everything – from horses to vines – is here for a purpose. Why are you surprised by it? Even the sun will tell you that it is here to do its job. So will all other gods. Why were *you* created? For pleasure? Does it stand up to common sense?

20. Whatever happens is natural

Nature has a purpose for everything – beginning, continuing, and ending – just like a ball thrown in the air. What does the ball gain when it goes up? Or lose when it comes down? What does a bubble gain when it is a bubble? Or lose when it bursts? Isn't this the same of a candle too?

21. Our world is just a dot in space

Turn your body inside out. What do you see? What about old age, sickness, or decay?

Those who praise and those who are praised. Those who remember and those who are remembered. All are all short-lived. How small is their place in this part of the

world! Yet, even here, they are not at peace with one another. The entire earth is just a point in space.

---

22. Be here now

Give your full attention to what is in front of you – an
object, an action, a principle, or the meaning of what
someone says.

You will be disappointed, and rightly so. If you choose
to become good tomorrow then be good today.

---

23. Serving humankind is accepting everything

Am I doing anything?
  I do it for the good of humankind.
  Does anything happen to me?
  I receive it as coming from the gods, from that univer-
sal source from which everything flows.

---

24. Life is like a bath

What do baths bring to mind?
  Oil, sweat, dirt, greasy water, all disgusting.
  Such is life and everything in it.

STOIC MEDITATIONS • 127

25. Every life ends

Death took Verus from Lucilla, then Lucilla herself. Maximus from Secunda, then Secunda herself. Diotimus from Epitynchanus, then Epitynchanus after him. Faustina from Antoninus and Antoninus in his turn. So it was with all of them. Celer buries Hadrian and is buried himself.

Where are they now – the noble-minded, the insightful, and the proud? Brilliant people like Charax, Demetrius the Platonist, Eudaemon, and others like him? All lasting just a day. All dead and gone now. Some forgotten as soon as dead, some became legends, and then faded legends.

So, remember that your complex body is also broken up one day and scattered. What makes it move will not be there anymore. It will be removed somewhere and transformed.

26. Delight is doing what you are made for

Your true delight lies in doing things you are made for. You are made to show goodwill to others, to rise above temptations, to distinguish appearances from reality, and to understand nature and how it works.

27. The three relationships

We have three relationships:

  i.   With our body that envelops us;
  ii. With the divine, that causes everything; and

iii.   With our fellow human beings.

---

28. No evil can touch you

Pain affects either the body or the soul. The body can speak for itself but the soul has the power to be serene and tranquil, choosing not to be affected. All our decisions, impulses, desires, or aversions come from within us. No evil can force its way here.

---

29. It is within your power to avoid evil

Erase all you imagine and keep telling yourself, "It is within my power to make sure that no evil, no lust, and no confusion finds a home in my soul. I have the power to see everything the way it is and deal with it accordingly." Remember, you have this authority. It is nature's gift to you.

---

30. Speak in the right tone

Speak in the right tone, without trying to impress, whether you are speaking in public or to someone in particular. Speak plainly.

---

31. Like every individual, every clan ends

Think of Augustus. His court, wife, daughter, children, grandchildren, sister, Agrippa, relatives, associates, friends, Areius, Maecenas, medical attendants, and priest – all vanished.

Think of others. Not the death of individuals but of the entire clan – the Pompeys, for example – and the writings on their tombstones: 'The last surviving descendant.' Think of all of their anxiety to have a successor to them, and yet, in the end, someone has to be the last. One more clan perished.

---

32. Let all actions contribute to a cohesive life

Everything you do should contribute to a cohesive life. Be happy if everything you do achieves its goal. No one can stop that.

"But others will interfere."

Not for behaving with justice, self-control, and fairness of your intentions.

"But still, they can prevent some of my practical actions."

Maybe, but if you face frustration with good grace and are sensible enough to accept what comes along, you may find an alternative course that is equally consistent with the cohesive life we are talking about.

---

33. Receive with humility. Let it go gracefully

Receive with humility. Let it go gracefully.

34. You can reunite with nature

Have you seen a severed hand or foot or head? That's what you are trying to do to yourself when you refuse to accept what happens, try to break away from society, or act selfishly. You have torn yourself away from the oneness of nature. You were born a part of it, and yet you have cut yourself away with your own hands.

Here is a beautiful thought. It is still in your power to reunite. God hasn't given this power to reunite a severed part with the whole to any other part of his creation. Look, then, how he has dignified human beings with his goodness. He has put it in their power not to be separated from the oneness of nature; but, when they separate, he allowed them to reunite and resume their place as before.

35. Setbacks are raw materials

The universal rational nature has given powers to rational beings. This was one of them: Nature uses every obstacle, every opposition, and works around it and makes it a part of itself; so too, a rational being can turn each setback as material to be used to achieve their goal.

36. Deal with things as they come up

Don't be confused by trying to imagine your life in its entirety. Don't try to imagine everything bad that could happen. Rather, as you face each one, ask yourself,

"What is so unbearable or intolerable about this?" You'll be embarrassed to answer.

Remember, it is neither the past nor the future that's weighing you down. It's only the present – even its effect can be minimised. All you need to do is keep it within its limits. Be firm in dealing with your mind if it finds it difficult to cope with such a small thing.

---

37. No one lives forever

Do Pantheia or Pergamus still sit by the tomb of Verus? Do Chabrias or Diotimus at the tomb of Hadrian? Ridiculous! Suppose that they did sit, would the dead be aware of it? If they were aware, would they be pleased? If they were pleased, would the mourners become immortal? Is it not their destiny to grow old and die? What would the emperors do when mourners die? All this is for the rotting meat in a bag.

---

38. If you've eyes to see, see clearly

As Crito, the philosopher says, "If you have eyes to see, then see clearly."

---

39. Human beings are naturally just

In the way human beings are made, I see no virtue placed in them to counter justice, but I see one to counter the love of pleasure: self-control.

40. Your opinion is the cause of pain

Take away your opinion of what is painful. You will find yourself perfectly secure.

"What is 'me'?"

Your reason.

"But I am not just reason."

So be it. Let the reason not trouble itself, then. If any other part of you suffers, let it have its own opinion about itself.

41. The mind is untouchable

For animals, anything that obstructs their senses or frustrates their aim is harmful. Plants can be similarly obstructed and harmed. In the same way, anything that frustrates the mind is harmful to the nature of the mind.

Apply this to yourself.

Does a pleasure or a pain affect you? Let your senses deal with that. Have you been frustrated in your path? If you had failed because you didn't make allowance for an obstacle, such an obstacle is harmful to you as a rational being.

However, once you understand the natural course of things, you are neither harmed nor frustrated. No one can harm or frustrate your mind. Fire, swords, oppression, slander, and everything else are powerless to touch it. "When it has been made a sphere, it continues a sphere."

42. Don't harm others – or yourself

I have no business causing pain to myself because I have not intentionally caused pain to anyone else.

43. Keep a clear mind

Different things delight different people. I find delight in keeping my reasoning mind clear. By not turning away from human beings and what happens to them. By seeing and accepting everything with kindness, dealing with them as they deserve.

44. Posthumous fame is meaningless

Make the best of the present. People who go after posthumous fame forget that future generations will also be mortal and no different from those who try our patience now. What difference does it make to you whether people who come after you make this sound or that?

45. Your soul remains unaffected

Lift me up and throw me, if you will. I will still have the divinity within me, serene and content, as long as I feel and act in accordance with nature.

Is there any reason why my soul should be affected by it, be made worse, be frightened, or be made spiritless? How could this possibly happen?

46. Whatever happens is bearable

Nothing happens to human beings that is not appropriate
to the nature of human beings. Nothing happens to an ox
that is not appropriate to the nature of an ox. Similarly
for a vine or a stone. If everything that happens is usual
or natural, why should you complain? The nature that is
common to all does not bring about anything unbearable.

47. Don't be pained by externals

If you are pained by anything external, the pain is not due
to the external thing. It is due to the way you look at it.
You have the power to change this at any moment.

If something in your character is causing pain, who
stops you from correcting it? If it is because you are not
doing anything to correct it, why don't you act instead of
complaining?

"But the obstacle is too big to overcome."

Don't worry then. It is not in your power to overcome
it.

"But life isn't worth living if this cannot be done."

Then bid life a contented farewell. Accept the frustration gracefully. Die like a human being in full activity
whose actions are not obstructed.

48. Take refuge in your inner citadel

Your ruling faculty is invincible when it withdraws into
itself. It calmly refuses to do anything against its will,

even if it may be totally irrational. Think how invincible it will be when based on reason and analysis.

A mind that is free from passion is a citadel. No place is more secure to seek protection and challenge attacks. Not to see this is ignorance. To see it, and yet not seek its refuge, is truly unfortunate.

49. Don't add your commentary

Never go beyond your first impressions. The first impressions tell you that so-and-so is speaking ill of you. That is their message. They did not tell you it has done you any harm. I see that my child is ill. My eyes tell me that, but they don't tell me that his life is in danger.

Always, then, keep the first impressions. Don't add anything of your own and you are safe. Or, add something – like someone who knows everything that happens in the world.

50. Nature is self-contained

Is the cucumber bitter? Throw it out. Are their briars in your path? Go around them. That's enough. Don't add, "Why are such things in the world?" The student of nature will laugh at you, just as a carpenter would if you find fault with sawdust at his place of work, or as a shoemaker would if you find fault with scraps of leather at his place.

They do have a place to dispose of these things, but nature has no external place like that. This is a wondrous thing about nature. Faced with the limitation, she takes everything that's worn-out, broken, and useless and re-fashions it into something new. So, nature needs no fresh supplies from outside. Neither does she need a place to throw out rubbish. She is content with her own space, her own material, and her own labour.

51. You are your own master

Avoid lazy actions, muddled speech, wandering thoughts, inner conflict, and outer gushing.

Don't be too busy in life to have leisure.

Suppose someone kills you, cuts you with a knife, or curses you. How can it affect your mind from being pure, wise, temperate, and just?

You may stand by a clear spring of sweet water and curse it, yet the wholesome spring water will keep on bubbling up. You may even throw mud and dirt into it, but it will quickly carry them away and will continue to be stainless.

How can you have a perpetual fountain (rather than a well) like that? By protecting your right to be your own master every hour of the day, with charity, simplicity, and modesty.

52. Don't seek the applause of the ignorant

- If you don't understand the nature of the universe, you cannot know *where* you are.

- If you don't understand the purpose of the universe, you cannot know what you are and *what* the universe is.
- If you don't understand either of these, you cannot know *why* you're here.

So, what we to make of anyone who cares for the applause of those who don't know where they are or what they are?

---

53. Avoid constant regrets

Do you want to be praised by people who curse themselves three times an hour? Those who despise themselves? How can people who regret nearly everything they do be happy?

---

54. Universal intelligence surrounds you

Let your intelligence be in harmony with the universal intelligence, just as your breath is in harmony with the air that surrounds you. Just as air is present everywhere, so is universal intelligence.

---

55. Only the perpetrator is harmed

The evil in the world cannot harm the universe. An individual's evil does not harm the victim. It harms no one but the person who is responsible for causing harm. He can free himself anytime he chooses.

56. You are the ruler of your domain

Other people's will is of no concern to me any more than their breath or their bodies. No matter how much we are made for one another, you rule your own domain. Otherwise, their evil will become your will. God doesn't want this because that would give someone else the power to ruin your happiness.

57. Transmit light like a sunbeam

The sunlight pours down on us and expands in all directions. Yet, it is never exhausted. This down-pouring is self-extension. Sunbeams derive their very name from the word signifying 'to be extended.' To understand the nature of a sunbeam, watch it as it streams into a dark room through a narrow opening. It travels in a straight line and stops when it faces a solid object that blocks it. It just rests there, without falling, without slipping.

That's how your thoughts should be.

- Not exhausting, but extending themselves;
- Not violently clashing against obstacles;
- Not falling away in despair.
  But,
- Holding the ground;
- Lighting up the thing upon which they rest.

When you don't transmit light, you create your own darkness.

58. Death is nothing to fear

If you fear death, you fear what you may experience: nothing at all but something different. If you feel nothing at all, it is no evil; if you feel something different, you are a new being and will continue to exist.

59. We are made for one another

We exist for one another. We make each other better or put up with each other.

60. The mind always moves straight ahead

An arrow travels in one way, but the mind in another. Even when the mind is cautious and is working around a problem from different angles, it still moves directly forward towards its goal.

61. Entering into others' minds

Entering into others' minds is letting them enter yours.

Book 9

Get Your Good from Yourself

1. Nature is indifferent but orderly

Injustice is a sin. Nature made rational beings for mutual benefit, to help, not harm, one another. To go against nature's will is to sin against the highest god.

Lying is also a sin against the same god. The universal nature is the nature of everything. All things are closely linked. Truth is just another name for this universal nature, the original creator of everything true. To lie deliberately is a sin because the liar is unjust. To lie involuntarily is also a sin because the liar disrupts the harmony of nature. It conflicts with the universal order. He received from nature the power to distinguish truth from falsehood, but he has neglected to distinguish between the two and now he cannot tell the difference.

It is a sin to pursue pleasure as a good and pain as an evil. You are bound to complain that nature is unfair in treating the good and the evil by letting the bad enjoy the pleasure and the good suffer pain. If you are afraid of pain, you are afraid something is bound to happen because of the nature of things. Again, this is a sin. When you pursue pleasure, you can hardly avoid being unjust, which is clearly a sin.

Nature is indifferent to some things. If it had a preference between two things, it wouldn't have created both. If we want to follow nature, we should have her mindset and share her indifference. To prefer life or death, pleasure or pain, fame or disrepute is a sin. Nature does not prefer one over the other.

What do I mean when I say that nature does not have a preference? I mean that everything happens indifferently, at different times, to the things that exist now, and to things to come later, through some ancient impulse of God. It is this impulse that moved from a certain beginning to the current order of things. It is the impulse that laid down the principles of what was to come in the future and gave them generative powers of change and existence – the power to progress from the beginning of the universe to its present orderly state.

---

2. Avoid all vices that damage humanity

A fine person would have said goodbye to this world before coming across falsehood, double-dealing, luxury, and pride. To die when you have had enough taste of these would be the second best thing. Or, have you decided to go on living in the midst of evil? Hasn't experience taught you to avoid it like the plague? In fact, an infection of mind is far more dangerous than anything you can contract from the polluted atmosphere. Diseases threaten our lives, but an infection of mind attacks our humanity.

---

3. Death is a natural process

Don't look down on death. Welcome it with a smile because it is one of those things that nature wills. Like youth and old age, like growth and maturing, like a new set of teeth, a beard, and grey hairs, like sex, pregnancy, and childbirth, like every other natural process at every stage of life, so is our ending.

A thoughtful person will not view death lightly, impatiently, or with disrespect. She will wait for it as one more of nature's processes. As one would wait for children to be born of a mother's womb, so one should wait for the soul to emerge from its container.

Perhaps you are looking for a simpler comfort that will appeal to you. There is no better comfort when you face death than to think of the conditions and the people you are leaving behind. There is no need to resent them. In fact, you must take care of them and treat them gently. Yet, don't forget that their principles are very different from yours. There is only this reason, if any, that would make us stay here: the chance to be friends with those who believe in similar principles.

However, when you look at how tiresome it is to live in the company of people with conflicting principles, it is enough to make you cry to death. "Come quickly, before I too forget who I am."

4. Your unjust actions harm you

When you cause harm, you harm yourself. When are unjust, you are unjust to yourself because you make yourself bad.

5. Sins of omission

You can also be unjust by not acting.

6. It is enough

It is enough if your opinion is based on understanding, your action on unselfishness, and your attitude on acceptance.

7. Let reason rule

Erase your imagination. Check your impulse. Reduce your appetites. Let reason rule supreme.

8. We all breathe the same air

Irrational animals are assigned one life principle and rational animals another. All earthly creatures share this one earth. All of us who see and breathe see the same light and breathe the same air.

9. We are attracted to other rational beings

All things are drawn towards others of the same kind: what is earthly towards earth, what is watery towards water, what is airy towards air. We need barriers to keep them forcibly separate. Flames, because of their nature, are drawn skyward, but they are ready for the company of their own kind even here. Any reasonably dry material will ignite easily – there are only a few things that are fire-resistant.

In the same way, all parts of the universal mind are drawn towards one another. In fact, even more strongly because they are higher in creation. Therefore, their tendency to blend and combine with their counterparts is greater. We can observe this instinct for reunion among irrational animals – bees swarming, cattle herding, birds nesting in colonies, and couples mating. Because they have souls, their bonding is developed, something you don't see in plants, stones, or trees.

When we come to rational beings, there are political associations, comradery, family, public meeting, treaties among nations, and armistices. In those things that are even more developed – such as the stars – a sense of unity exists even when they are separated from one another by huge distances. The higher the order of creation, the greater the attraction, even when things are far from one another.

Yet, see what happens. It is we, the rational beings, who have lost the sense of attraction to our fellow beings by not allowing the currents to converge. Human beings may try to flee as they will, but nature is stronger. It will catch and hold them fast. Observe, and you will see. It is easier to see a fragment of earth away from earth than to see a human being with no connection to fellow human beings.

10. Reason bears fruit

Everything bears fruit: human beings, God, the whole universe. Each fruit has its season. Normally we limit the word to plants like vines. Reason too bears fruit, both for itself and for the world. From it comes the harvest of other good things, all in turn bearing the stamp of reason.

11. Be kind to those who know no better

Teach them better if you can. If not, remember, kindliness has been given to you for times like these. The gods themselves are patient with them and even help them in their efforts to gain health, wealth, and reputation. This you could do too. What is stopping you?

12. Work hard as a rational being

Work hard – not feeling like a victim, not for gaining sympathy or admiration, but for just this: what you do or don't do should be worthy of a rational being.

13. Your opinions cause your troubles

Today, I've got out of all troubles. Rather, I got them out of me because they were within me, in my opinions.

14. Nothing is different

Everything is the same, familiar in experience, fleeting in duration, and worthless in content. Everything now is just as it was in the time of those who we buried.

15. The reasoning mind judges things

Things stand outside of us. They are what they are and nothing more. They know nothing about themselves, and they don't pass any judgment upon themselves.

What judges them, then?

Your reasoning mind.

16. Will, not feelings, decide good and bad

The rational and social animals are not made better or worse by what they feel but by how they decide to act. It is like a person's outward behaviour, which is – whether good or bad –the product of their will, not of their feelings.

17. Up or down, makes no difference

A stone thrown in the air loses nothing by coming down. Neither did it gain anything by going up.

18. No one is perfect

Enter the minds of your critics. You will see what kind of people you were afraid of and how they judge themselves.

19. All things are changing

All things are changing. You yourself are continuously transforming. Some parts of you are decaying, and so is the whole universe.

20. Leave other people's mistakes where they are

Leave other people's wrongdoing where it lies.

21. Change is not terrible

There is no evil in interrupting or discontinuing an activity, which is, in a sense, their death. It doesn't harm us. Now think about your childhood, youth, adulthood, and old age. Every change is a form of death. Was that so terrible? Or, think of your life with your grandfather, your mother, and then your father. Think of the deaths, changes, and endings in those days. Ask yourself: Was that so terrible? Then neither will the end and transformation of your life be.

22. Recognize the similarity of minds

Be ready to explore your mind, the mind of the universe, and your neighbour's mind.

- Your own, so you can make it just;
- The universe's, so you can understand your part; and
- Your neighbour's, so you know if they are informed by knowledge or by ignorance.

Recognize it as similar to yours.

23. You are a unit of society

You help complete society as one of its units. So also, every one of your actions should help complete the social life. Any action not directed toward a social end (either directly or indirectly) disturbs your life and destroys its wholeness, like a person in a popular assembly, standing alone against the general agreement.

24. Everything repeats

[Such is everything:] Childish quarrels, childish games, 'spirits carrying dead bodies'. What is represented in the mansion of the dead is clear to us now.

25. See things without their material part

First, understand the quality of an object. Then detach it from its material part and study it. Think about how long it will last.

26. Let reason do its job

You have had many problems, all because you didn't let reason, your guide and master, do its natural work. Enough. No more.

27. Help everyone as the gods do

When someone hates or blames you, when someone says harmful things about you, look at their soul. See what manner of people they are. You will find that you don't need to bother to impress them, yet you must be kind to them. By nature, they are friends. The gods themselves help them every step of the way, by dreams, by signs, to get what they want.

28. Things are forever changing

The world's cycle never changes. Up and down from age to age.

It may be that the universe's intelligence sets itself into motion for each separate thing. If so, accept whatever the result is. Or, it puts itself into motion once and everything follows in sequence. Every event creates the one that follows.

To put it in another way, they are either isolated happenings or a single unified one. If it is an aimless chance, then you are also a part of it. [What is there to worry about?]

Soon the earth will cover us all. Then the earth itself will change. Things that result from the change will also change, and change they will forever. And, these again forever. If you think about the waves of swiftly rolling changes, you will not value mortal things.

---

29. The task of philosophy is modest

The universal cause is like a flood, sweeping everything along with it. How foolish are these people who play at politics and convince themselves that they are philosophers! Babes, incapable of wiping their noses!

Well, then what? Do what nature demands now. Get moving and don't look around to see if anyone is looking at you. Don't go expecting Plato's Republic. Be satisfied, if even with the smallest progress. Count the result as no small success. After all, who can change a person's convictions? Without a change of conviction, what can be there except slavery of those who groan while pretending to obey?

Go on, then, talk to me about Alexander, Philip, Demetrius of Phalerum. It is for them to say whether they knew nature's will and made themselves its students.

But, if they were just play acting the role of heroes, no one condemned me to imitate them.

The task of philosophy is modest – all simplicity and plain-dealing. Don't tempt me into audacity and pride.

30. Fame and reputation are worthless

Look down from above on thousands of humans, their rituals, their voyages in storm and calm, and the differences among those who are born, who live together, and who die.

Consider the lives of those who lived a long time ago, the lives of those not yet born, the lives we live even now, and the lives of savages in a far-off land. How many even know your name? How many will have forgotten it soon? How many, who perhaps praise you now, will soon abuse you? Therefore, to be remembered is worthless. So is fame or anything else.

31. Common good is according to nature

Be indifferent to external events. Be just and fair in your actions. In short, let the common good guide your thoughts and actions. This is according to nature.

32. Let go of anxieties

You can get rid of many of the anxieties that disturb you now. They are just your opinion. Let your mind become spacious by

- Allowing your thoughts to embrace the universe
- Contemplating the eternity
- Thinking about the speed with which things change
- Considering the short span between life and death
- The boundless time before birth
- The boundless time after death.

33. All things pass quickly

All that you see now will be gone quickly. Those who see their going will go the same way before long. Then what is there to choose between the oldest grandfather and the baby that died in its cradle?

34. You are not hurt by others

Observe these people – their principles, what they struggle for, and what they like and value. Picture their souls laid bare. They imagine their praise and blame can help others, or hurt others. How presumptuous!

35. Nature orders everything the right way

Loss is nothing but change, but nature delights in change. Since the universe began and to this day, things have been ordered by her will. It will continue to be so in the endless future. How, then, can you say that things have always been and will be bad? And, that no god can set this right and the world has been condemned to be bound by evil?

36. Everything decays

We are made of stuff that is bound to decay: water, dust, bone, and filth. Marble rocks are nothing but bumps on the earth; gold and silver are her sediments; the garments, a bit of her hair; purple dye, shellfish blood. So, it is with everything else. So, is the very breath of our lives – changing from this to that.

37. Become a simpler and better person

Enough of this miserable, whining, monkey life. Why are you so disturbed? None of this is new. Why are you shaken? The way it looks? Take a look at it. The substance of it? Look at that too. Beyond the form and the matter, there's nothing else.

Even at this late hour try to become a simpler and better person in the eyes of the gods. For mastering that lesson, three years are as good as one hundred.

38. Don't worry about others' wrongs

If anyone has done anything wrong, it is their sin. But, probably they didn't do anything wrong.

39. No need to be disturbed

There are two possibilities.

One, all things spring from one intelligent source and fall into place to make up one body. In this case, no part should complain about what happens to the good of the whole.

Two, the world is nothing but atoms and their confused mixing and dispersing. So why be troubled?

Say to reason that rules you, "Are you dead? Decaying? Are you just playing a role? Have you become an animal, grazing, and herding with the rest?"

40. Pray for the strength to face what happens

The gods have the power, or they don't. If they don't, why pray at all? If they do, instead of praying for things to happen or not to happen, why not pray to feel fear or desire or grief? Clearly, if they can help us at all, they help us this way.

"But the gods put those things in my power."

Then why don't you use what is in your power to be a free human being? Why be a slave of things not in your power? Besides, who told you the gods won't help you even with things in your power? Begin praying this way and you'll see:

- Not "let me sleep with the person," but, "let me not lust after this person."

- Not "let me be rid of this person," but, "let me not be desperate to be rid of this person."
- Not "let me not lose my son," but, "let me not be terrified of losing him."

Pray this way. See what happens.

---

41. Focus on what's in front of you, even in sickness

Epicurus said, "When I was sick, I didn't waste my visitors' time by talking about my physical condition. Instead, I talked about natural philosophy and, in particular, this: how the mind can be a part of the feelings of the body and yet be serene and pursue its own good. I didn't give the doctors a chance to brag about their cures. My life just went on normally, smoothly, and happily."

Be like that in sickness or in any other situation. Never give up philosophy, no matter what happens. Don't get into arguments with the ignorant and uninformed (as any school of philosophy would agree). Focus fully on doing what is in front of you and the resources you have to accomplish that.

---

42. Be kind for its own sake

When you are offended by someone's shameless behaviour, ask yourself, "Can there be a world without shameless people?" No, it is not possible. So, don't ask for what is impossible. Such people are necessarily a part of this world, so are the vicious, untrustworthy, or those with other character flaws. When you realise that they *have to* exist, you become more kind towards them.

It is also helpful to remember what resources nature has given us to cope with such faults. Nature has indeed given us many antidotes, such as gentleness to meet brutality and other antidotes for other ills.

Generally speaking, you can try to set them straight because anyone who does wrong is doing something the wrong way.

Besides, how did it harm you anyway? None of those who you are hurt by can damage your mind, which is the only harm. So, what is surprising or wrong about boors behaving boorishly? Shouldn't you rather blame yourself for not anticipating that they would behave this way? You are a rational being and had the means of knowing that it is likely that they would behave this way. You forgot, and now you are surprised. Whenever you think of someone as untrustworthy or ungrateful, turn your thoughts to yourself. It is clearly *your* mistake if you thought that such people would behave in any other way or to show kindness expecting something in return, instead of being kind because it is its own reward.

Once you have done someone a service, what more do you want? Aren't you happy enough that you followed the laws of nature? Are you also expecting to be paid for it? That's like the eye expecting a reward for seeing, or the feet for walking. That's what they are made for. They do their part by doing what they were created to do.

Similarly, a human being is born to be kind. When you have done something kind or something else for the

CHUCK CHAKRAPANI

common good, you have done what you are made for.
You get what is your own.

BOOK 10

A Healthy Mind Can Face Anything

1. Be fit for the company of the gods

My soul, will you ever be good, simple, whole, all open, as plain to see as the body that surrounds you? Will you never enjoy the sweetness of a loving and affectionate heart? Will you never be fulfilled, wanting nothing from people or things? Or, more time to enjoy them? Or, enjoy them in a more pleasant climate? Or, for people who are easier to get along with?

When will you be content with what you have now, happy knowing you have everything and everything comes from the gods? All is and will be well with you so long as the gods decide and have in store for you the preservation of the perfect living being – the good, just, and beautiful. It creates and holds together all things; it contains and embraces all things that are dissolved so other things like them can be created.

Will you ever be fit for such fellowship with the gods and humans, so you neither blame them nor be condemned by them?

2. Pay attention to nature's demands

Pay attention to what your nature asks of you as if you are governed by it only. Do it and accept it unless it harms your physical nature. Then you pay attention to that physical nature and accept that too, unless it harms your rational and social nature. Follow these rules. Don't waste time on other things.

3. You can endure anything

Nature has prepared you to face anything that happens, or she hasn't. Therefore,

- If something bearable happens, don't resent it. Nature has enabled you to bear it.
- If something unbearable happens, still don't resent it. It will destroy itself after destroying you.

But, remember, nature has given you the ability to endure anything you think you can. Treat it so in your own self-interest.

4. Blame no one

If someone is mistaken, gently show them where they went wrong. If you fail, blame yourself. Better still, blame no one.

5. Whatever happens is meant to happen

Whatever happens to you has been waiting to happen since the beginning of time. You and the incident are woven in the spinning thread of cause and effect.

6. You are a part of the whole

Whether the universe is a confusion of atoms or nature, let your first conviction be this: you are part of the whole controlled by nature. And, the second, you have a relationship with other similar parts. If you bear these two thoughts in mind, you won't be unhappy with whatever you are assigned by the whole. What benefits the whole cannot harm the parts, and the whole doesn't do anything that is harmful to itself. While all natures share this common principle, the nature of the universe has a second principle: no outside force can harm it either.

By remembering that I am part of such whole, I will cheerfully accept whatever happens. Because I am related to the other parts whose nature is similar to mine, I will do nothing unsocial. Instead, I will join them, keep them in view, direct my actions towards their good and away from the opposite.

In doing so, my life will flow smoothly. As smoothly as the life of a citizen who acts for the benefit of her fellow citizens and is content with whatever task her city may assign to her.

7. Everything undergoes change

Everything that is naturally combined to create the universe must necessarily decay. Rather, they must undergo a change of form. If this is harmful to the parts but is unavoidable, then it is hard to see how the universe can run smoothly. Parts will change from one state to another, all built to be destroyed in different ways.

Did nature deliberately mean to harm things that are a part of itself? Did it make them vulnerable or even doom them? Or, could these things happen without nature knowing anything about them? Neither of the two makes sense.

Suppose we say that the inherent properties of nature account for these things and explain all this in terms of the normal order of creation. It is still absurd to say that the individual things are prone to change and yet be surprised and complain that it is 'contrary to nature', especially when things return to the state they came from. Our elements either are dispersed or change from solid to earth-form, airy to air-form. They are then absorbed into the universal Reason, whether they are periodically consumed by fire or renewed through continual change.

Don't imagine that the solid and the airy parts have been with you since you were born. They became a part of you yesterday or the day before, through the air you breathed and the food you ate. What changes is not what your mother gave birth to, but something you received since then.

Even if birth implicates us very much in the other part that is subject to change, my arguments still stand[36].

---

8. Be rational, tranquil, and high-minded

Once you consider yourself to be good, modest, truthful, rational, tranquil, and high-minded, don't trade them for other qualities. Don't let go of them. If you lose them, quickly return to them.

The term *rational* signifies an understanding of each individual thing, without neglect. The term *tranquil* means cheerfully accepting whatever you are assigned by nature. *High-minded* means rising above the sensations of the body and all other things like fame and death. If you maintain these qualities, whether others recognise it or not, you will become a new person leading a new life.

But, if you continue to be the person you are now, in a life that is in turmoil and degradation, you are indeed a very stupid person, much too fond of life. You are like an animal fighter in a game, covered with blood and bruises, yet wanting to fight again tomorrow, though you will be exposed to the same thing all over again.

So, come aboard this little boat with this handful of qualities and sail to the Island of the Blessed. If you start drifting and are unable to hold your course, find a quiet haven where you will be able to hold your own, or leave life completely – not in anger, but simply, freely, unassumingly, knowing that at least you have that much to your credit.

As you try to keep these qualities in mind, it will help a great deal to remember the gods. They have no desire to be flattered; all they want is that all rational beings be like them.

And, remember, what does the work of a fig tree is a fig tree, what does the work of a dog is a dog, what does the work of a bee is a bee, and what does the work of human being is a human being.

9. Hold on to your sacred principles

Wipe out your sacred principles: frivolity, fighting, cowardice, laziness, and flattery. What does duty require?

- To observe every single thing;
- To exercise the powers of thought;
- To perform each action, making sure that it fulfills the practical demands of the situation; and
- Maintain a quiet self-confidence of someone who has mastered the details.

When are you going to attain happiness based on integrity and dignity? Or, gain an understanding of each individual thing – its place in the world-order, its life-span, its make-up, who it belongs to, and who has the power to give it or take it away?

10. Conquerors are robbers

Spiders are proud of catching flies. Men are proud of catching hares, fish, wild boars, bears, or Sarmatians[37]. Examine their principles. Are they not robbers?

11. Become a student of change

Acquire the ability to see how one thing changes into another. Constantly observe it. Use it to train yourself. Nothing will elevate your mind more because you realise that, at any moment, you may have to leave everything behind you, including the company of your friends and relatives. From then on, you dedicate yourself wholly to the service of justice in whatever you do and nature in everything else. What people think or say or do against you is no longer your concern. Only two questions concern you now:

- Is what you are doing the right thing to do?
- Do you gladly accept whatever is given to you?

All your cares and distractions are gone. You only want to walk the straight path of (the divine) law. By doing so, you become the follower of God.

12. Follow reason

Why be suspicious and fearful? You can see clearly what you need to do. If you see the road clearly, follow it. Don't turn back. If not, wait for the best advice you can get. If you face hurdles, keep advancing to the best of your ability. Stick to what seems just and right. Always try to achieve this and, if you fail, don't be discouraged in attempting to do this.

If you follow reason in all things, you will be both tranquil and active at the same time, and cheerful and collected as well.

13. Don't worry about what others think

When you wake up, ask yourself: would it make any difference to you if others blame you for doing what is just and right?

Of course, not.

Have you forgotten that people who arrogantly praise and blame others do the same in their private lives as they sleep and eat? Have you forgotten what they do, what they avoid, what they go after, how they steal and rob? They don't do it with their feet and hands but with that most precious of all possessions, which is the source of faith, truth, order, and well-being.

14. Accept nature's will

Nature gives everything and takes everything away. A modest person will tell her, "Give what you like. Take away what you like," not with pride but with obedience and goodwill.

15. Live as though on a mountain top

You have only a few more years left. Live them, then, as though on a mountain top. It makes no difference whether you live here or there if you live anywhere as though it is your city. Let people see and let them know how someone lives according to nature. If they cannot stand it, let them kill you. It is better that way than to live like them.

16. Don't talk about being good; be good

Don't waste time arguing what a good person should be. Be one.

17. The immensity of time and substance

Constantly think about all of the time and all of substance. Each separate thing is a grain of sand compared to all substance, a turn of a screw in eternity.

18. Everything that is born dies

Understand that all material things are already undergoing change, decay, or dispersion. Everything that is born dies.

19. Pretensions of people

See what people are when they are eating, sleeping, mating, easing themselves, and the rest. Then see how pompous, arrogant, overbearing, and angry they are from their high position. A moment ago, they were licking many feet, and for what? A moment from now, they will do it again.

20. Nature brings what is good

Nature brings what is good for everyone and everything, and at the precise moment.

21. I love what the universe loves

Earth is in love with the showers from above,
And all-holy Heaven itself is in love.[38]

The universe loves to create the next thing. I tell the universe, "I love what you love." (Isn't what we mean we say 'such-and-such thing loves happening'?)

22. Be cheerful

- You continue to live here, as you are used to; or
- You go away of your own free will; or
- You die, which means your service has ended.

What else is there besides these? So be cheerful.

23. All places are the same

Let this always be clear to you. Where you are now is like any other place. All things here are the same as on the mountain top, on the seashore, or wherever you choose to be. As Plato says, it is like 'making the city walls like a shepherd's fold on a mountain.'

24. Watch your ruling faculty

What is my ruling faculty to me? What am I making of it now? What am I using it for? Is it empty of understanding? Is it loose and isolated from others? Has it melted and merged and so identified with the flesh that shares its urges?

25. Giving in to anger is to be a fugitive

A slave who runs away from his master is a fugitive. For us, the law is the master. To break away from it is being a fugitive. Grief, anger, and fear are rejections of something that has been dictated in the past, the present, or the future by the power that directs the universe. It is the law, which assigns every creature its due. So, to give in to grief, fear, or anger is to become a fugitive.

26. Observe the hidden force

Someone deposits his sperm and leaves. Then another force takes it, works on it, and creates a child. What a transformation!

He puts food down his throat, and another force takes it over, and converts into sensation and motion and, in short, life, strength, and other things. How many and how strange!

Observe these things that are produced in hidden ways. See the power that carries things up and down, not with your eyes, but just as clearly with your reason.

27. The same performance, different actors

Bear this in mind always. All the life of today is a repetition of the past, and it will repeat in the future. See the many dramas and their settings. All so similar. You have known them from your own experience or from history: Hadrian or the courts of Antoninus or the courts of

Philip, Alexander, and Croseus. The same performance. Different actors.

28. Voluntarily follow what happens

When you see someone annoyed or resentful of something, picture them as the pig at the sacrifice, kicking and squealing all the way. Another who silently weeps in his bed over the chains that bind him is no better.

Everything has to submit to what happens, but only rational beings are given the power to follow what happens voluntarily.

29. Fear of losing and fear of dying

Whatever you do, ask yourself every step of the way, "Am I afraid of death because I might lose this?"

30. We are all compelled in our behaviour

When you are offended by someone's behaviour, turn around and ask why *you* have acted like that. Do you find good in riches, pleasure, reputation, and things like that? Think that way and you will soon forget your anger when you realise that they acted under compulsion. What else could they do? If you can, take away the compulsion.

STOIC MEDITATIONS • 171

31. Everything is raw material for reason[39]

- When you see Satyron, think of (the dead) Socratius or Eutyches, or Hyman.
- When you see Alciphron, see Tropaeophorus.
- When you see Servus, see Crito or Xenophon.
- When you look at yourself, think of all emperors that went before you.
- When you see anyone, think of their counterparts.

Where are they now? Nowhere. Or no one knows where.

This way you will get used to looking on that human life as vapour and nothingness, especially when you remember that, once things change, they cease to exist forever.

Then why struggle and strain? Why not be content to live your short life in the right way?

Think of the opportunities – the raw materials for the good – you are rejecting. What is any of this but training for your reason, once you examine the nature of things that happen in life carefully?

So, keep at it, until you make these things your own – just like a blazing fire makes flame and brightness out of everything you throw at it.

32. Live right or depart

Let no one have the right to say truthfully that you are without integrity or goodness. Should anyone think so, see that they have no basis. All depends on you. Who else can stop you from attaining goodness and integrity? If you cannot live that, decide not to go on living, Not even reason will ask you to do otherwise.

33. Derive pleasure by following nature

What is the very best we can say or do with the material we are made of? Whatever it is, it is in your power to say or do it. Don't pretend that you are not free to do it.

You will never stop complaining until your mind feels the same pleasure from doing what is proper for human being to do (given the circumstances, inherent or accidental) that a he donist gets from self-indulgence,. You should consider that everything you do in accordance with nature is a pleasure, and you can do this anywhere.

A cylinder cannot move at will. It can only move in its own motion. Neither can water, fire, or anything else that is governed by its nature or is a soul without reason. Many things stand in their way, but intelligence and reason can make their way through any obstacle. Their nature and will make it possible. Keep before your eyes the ease with which reason carries through all things – as a fire upwards, as a stone downwards, as a cylinder down a slope. Be content. Ask no more.

All other obstacles can either affect the body only, which is a dead thing, or have no power to crush or injure us unless we help them with our preconceptions and surrender our reason. If they did, anyone who felt it would be immediately degraded. We know that, throughout the rest of creation, any harm makes them worse. Yet, in the case of human beings, we can even say that they become better and more praiseworthy by using adversity in the right way.

Finally, remember that nothing harms an individual if it does not harm the community. Nothing harms the community if it does not harm the law. What we call misfortunes do not injure law and therefore cannot harm the community or the individual.

---

34. Internalize the precepts

When you have internalised true principles, even the briefest reminder is enough. It will remind you to be free from grief and fear.

Leaves, some the wind scatters on the ground –

So is the race of men[40]

You children are leaves. Leaves are those who talk platitudes, curse, sneer, and scoff. Leaves are also those who loyally applaud and praise you even after you die. All these are produced like flowers in springtime. The wind blows them away, and soon the forest produces other leaves in their place.

All our lives are brief. And yet, you go after life or shrink away from it, as though it is going to last forever. A short time and you'll close your eyes. The one who buries you will be mourned soon enough.

35. A healthy mind can face anything

A healthy pair of eyes should see everything in sight and not wish for just a green colour. It is a symptom of a diseased eye. Likewise, healthy hearing should hear all kinds of sounds, healthy smells all kinds of scents, healthy stomachs all kinds of foods, like a mill that accepts all kinds of grist.

In the same way, a healthy mind should be prepared to face whatever happens. A mind that says, "Let my children live," or, "Let everyone praise everything I do," is an eye that wants to see only green or teeth that only want to eat mush.

36. Follow nature's ways

No man is so fortunate that there will be someone by his death bed who will be pleased with his passing. Let's say you are virtuous and wise. Still, there will be someone who says, "Finally! We can breathe freely again without our master! Sure, he was not harsh to us, but he certainly had silent contempt for us. " That's what happens to a good person. What about the rest of us? How many good reasons are there to make some of our friends happy to get rid of us? Think of this when the time comes. You will leave more contented if you say to yourself, "I'm leaving such a life, in which even my companions on whose behalf I worked so hard, prayed, and cared for want me gone. And, they hope to derive some benefit out of it. How can anyone, then, want to stay here longer?"

Yet, don't be less kind to them when you leave because of this. Maintain your usual friendliness, goodwill, and charity. Let your departure not be unwillingly forced. Let your departure be an easy one. Let your soul easily glide away from the body.

Once nature tied you to others and made you one of them. Now she's untying you. I am separated from my folks, unresisting and unforced. It's one of nature's ways.

37. Understand the 'why' behind all actions

"Why is this person doing this?" is the question you should ask yourself whenever someone – including yourself – does something.

38. What pulls your strings is hidden

Remember, what pulls your strings is hidden deep within you. This is the power of persuasion; this is life. One can even say this is the human being. Don't confuse it with flesh and other organs that surround it. Except for the fact that they are attached to you from birth, they are no more than instruments like an axe. These are useless without what moves and holds them, like the weaver's shuttle, the writer's pen, or a driver's whip.

BOOK 11

Learn the Art of Living

1. A rational soul is self-aware

These are the properties of a rational soul: It sees itself, analyses itself, and makes of itself whatever it chooses. It enjoys its own fruit (unlike fruit produced by trees or the counterpart produced by animals, which are enjoyed by others). It always completes its work no matter where the limit of its life is set.

If events such as dances or plays are cut short, they will be considered incomplete, but the soul reaches its completion no matter where it is stopped, and it can say, "I have completed my purpose."

It surveys the entire universe, the void that is surrounding it, and the way they are put together. It extends itself into the infinity of time, and understands and accepts the periodic births and rebirths of all things. It sees that the future generations will see nothing new. Those who went before us hadn't anything more than we do now either. The past generations saw nothing more than we do. Anyone who has lived forty years with any understanding at all has virtually seen – thanks to their similarities – both the past and the future.

This is also the property of the rational soul: love of one's neighbours, truthfulness, and modesty, as well as not placing anything above itself (also a characteristic of law). Thus, the right reason does not differ at all from the principle of justice.

2. Resist seduction by looking closely

You can soon learn to ignore the lure of a song, dance, and athletic performance.

- Break down the melody into several sounds and ask for each sound, "Is this what I can't resist?" You will be too embarrassed to admit it.
- Do the same for dance movements or the attitude of the dancers.
- Do the same with athletic performances.

Except for virtue and acts of virtue, remember to apply this method of breaking down seductive things into several parts and see that there is very little value in them.

Now, apply this method to life as a whole.

3. The soul is ready for anything, any time

Any time the call comes, the happy soul is ready to face separation from the body, death, dispersion, or survival. This readiness is its own decision and not in response to

outside forces (like the Christians). It has to be deliber-
ate, dignified, and persuasive without being reckless.[41]

4. Never stop doing good

Have you done something for the common good? Well
then, that's your reward. Keep this thought always in
mind. Never stop doing good.

5. Your profession is to be good

What's your profession? To be good, but how are you to
achieve it, unless you have a philosopher's insight into
the universe and into the nature of human beings?

6. Stage plays and their purpose

Tragedies were first brought on the stage to remind us
how things like this can happen naturally. If you are de-
lighted by what you saw on the stage, you shouldn't be
troubled with what takes place in the real world. We are
shown in these plays that consequences inevitably follow
actions. People can still bear them, despite their crying
out, "O Cithaeron![42]"

Some excellent things are said well by writers of dramas. For example, this:

Me and my children if the gods neglect

This has its reason too.

Or,

We must not chafe and fret at that which happens.

Or again,

Like the ears of corn, the lives of men are reaped.

And many other sayings of that nature.

Then came the Old Comedy, which had dignified freedom of speech. By its simplicity, it rebuked pride. It is for this reason that Diogenes adopted this style.

Then came the Middle Comedy, and then the New Comedy. They gradually degenerated into mimicry. As we all know, even these writers also had something good to say, but what does it all the poetry and the drama amount to?[43]

---

7. This is the time to practice philosophy

No other condition in life is as well suited for the practice of philosophy as the one you happen to be in right now. How plain this is to see!

---

8. Of the same tree, not of the same mind

A branch cut off from a connecting branch is also cut off from the whole tree. Similarly, human beings cut off from their fellow human beings are cut off from the whole community.

While a branch is cut off by someone else, people cut themselves off from the community. They turn away from others because of hatred and do not realise that they have cut themselves off from the community as well. Yet, God who formed this community have given us this power: we can grow again and reattach ourselves to the whole. But, if it happens often, it makes the reconnection more difficult. A branch that has never been severed from the beginning is not like the one that has been severed and reconnected. As gardeners say, it is of the same tree, but not of the same mind.

9. Be kind to those who obstruct you

Others may stand in your way when you follow the path of reason, but they won't be able to stop you from taking sound action. Don't let them stop you from being kind to them. Be on guard on both matters – not only in being steady in judgment and action but in being kind to those who stand in your way or cause you trouble otherwise.

It is a weakness to be angry with them as much as it is to abandon your course of action and give way to fear. In either case, you are deserting your post of duty, in one case, out of fear and in the other, out of alienation from your natural brothers and friends.

10. All virtues depend on justice

Nature is never inferior to art since art is no more than an imitation of nature. Nature, which is most perfect and all-inclusive, cannot fall short of the artificial in its crafts-manship. All arts do the inferior things for the sake of the superior. So, does the universal nature. Here then we find the origins of justice. All other virtues depend on it.

We can never achieve true justice if we go after mid-dle [indifferent] things, are or easily deceived or careless and changeable.

11. Avoid pursuing and avoiding

It may be that the things you pursue and avoid don't come to you; rather, you go to them. Don't judge them and they will be quiet. Then you will neither pursue nor avoid them.

12. The soul at rest is radiant

The soul maintains its figure as a sphere by not grasping at things beyond it or retreating inward. Not extended, not shrunk. She reveals herself to the world as radiant.

13. Hold no grudge or complaints

Does someone despise me? That's their problem. Mine is to ensure that what I do or say does not deserve be to sneered at.

Does someone hate me? Again, it is their problem. My job is to be friendly and charitable to everyone, including those who hate me, and show them their mistake. Not by rebuking them or making a show of my self-control, but frankly and honestly – assuming no pretension on my part – like the great Phocion.[44]

That is what we should be like inside. We should never let the gods catch us holding a grudge or complaining.

What harm can come to you as long as you do things that are in accordance with your nature and accept what the nature of the universe brings you? You are a human being who is placed at your post to advance the common good.

---

14. What we want is not what we do

They flatter one another, yet they despise one another. They want to be above one another, yet they crouch before one another.

---

15. Don't say you're honest; be honest

How hollow and insincere it sounds when someone says, "I am going to be honest with you." What are you doing? You don't have to give notice. It should be written on your face. It should echo in your voice. It should shine in your eyes. It should be like a single glance of a lover that is easily read by the beloved.

A person who is sincere and honest should exactly be like someone who has a strong smell. When you come near, you know it, but false honesty is like a knife in the back. Nothing is more disgraceful than a false friendship.

Avoid it at all costs. If you are truly good and sincere, it will show in your looks. No one can fail to see it.

16. Be indifferent to things that makes no difference

You can achieve the good life to perfection if you understand this: be indifferent to what makes no difference. You can do this by looking at each thing separately and then all things together. Remember that none of them is responsible for your opinion of it. They don't come to you but remain where they are. It is you who judge them and engrave them in your mind. It is in your power not to engrave anything at all in your mind or quickly delete anything that is engraved by accident. You need to do this only for a short time and then life will be over.

Besides, why is it a problem? If they are in accordance with nature, accept them gladly and it will be easy for you. If they are not, find out what your nature requires and follow that, even when it is not good for your reputation You are allowed to seek your own good.

17. Things change but suffer no harm

Think about where things come from, what they are made of, what they change into, and what they are going to be after they change. They will have suffered no harm.

18. Nine things to consider when offended

[If someone offends you, consider these first.]

One. What is my relationship to others? We are made for one another. In another sense, I am their guardian, as the ram is to a flock and as the bull is to the herd. Let's go back to the first principles. If it is not just atoms, the universe must be governed by nature. If this is so, lower creations must exist for the higher and the higher for each other.

Two. What kind of people are they while eating, sleeping, and so on? How driven are they by what they believe and how proud are they of it?

Three. If what they are doing is right, you have no reason to be annoyed. If it is not right, they do it unintentionally and out of ignorance. No soul is denied the truth deliberately, so no one ever denies others what they are entitled to. See how angry they become if you call them unjust, ungrateful, greedy, or any such thing that suggests that they aren't good neighbours.

Four. You have done many things wrong yourself. You are no different from them. You may avoid some mistakes, but you still have the potential to commit them. You just have not acted on it because of cowardice, or because you are concerned about your reputation, or for some other mean motive.

Five. You don't even know for sure that they did anything wrong. You cannot know for sure what motivated them. You need to know a lot more before you can correctly judge other people's actions.

Six. If you are too angry or impatient, remind yourself that this life lasts only a moment. After that, we are all laid to rest.

Seven. It is not what others do that bothers us. They do what they do as a result of *their* reasoning. What bothers us is the spin we put on their actions. Take away the spin. Don't judge their actions as something terrible. Your anger is gone. How do you do that? By understanding that someone else's action cannot shame you. If only shameful things are bad, you would be guilty of some bad things – robbery or who knows what else.

Eight. Our anger and annoyance cause us more damage than things that cause anger and annoyance.

Nine. Kindness is irresistible, as long as it is sincere and not a phoney act with a smile. Even the most vicious person can do nothing if you continue to treat him kindly and try to correct him gently when you get a chance. At the moment he tries to harm you, you say, "No, my friend. We are not made for this. You are not harming me, but you're harming yourself." Show him gently and courteously how this is so. Bees and animals that are made to be gregarious don't do this. When you say such things, don't be sarcastic or reprimanding, but with affection and with no hatred in your heart. Do not lecture for the admiration of others. Even if others are present, act as though you are dealing with him only.

Remember these nine rules as if you received them as a gift from the muses. As long as you live, be a human being. Do not be angry or flatter others. Both are selfish and harmful. In moments of anger, remember that there is nothing human about it. There is more humanity in courtesy and kindness. The person who has these qualities possesses strength, nerve, and courage, not someone in fits of anger and discontent. The freer your mind is from passions, the closer it is to strength. Anger is as much a sign of weakness as a sense of pain. In both cases, you receive a wound and feel defeated.

Ten. Here's a tenth gift from the leader of the Muses, Apollo: To expect bad people not to wrong is crazy. You are asking for the impossible. To let them offend others and yet expect that them not to offend you is irrational and arbitrary.

---

19. Handling the four lapses of rationality

There are four main lapses of your rational faculty. Guard against these at all times. If you catch them, wipe them out by reminding yourself

  i.   This thought is unnecessary.
 ii.   This thought is destructive to your fellowship.
iii.   This is not your true thought (it is out of place because it does not come from your heart.)
 iv.   When you are tempted to blame yourself, your divine part is beaten by your body, the inferior and perishable part.

---

20. Every element obeys the laws of nature

The air and the fire that are parts of you have a tendency to rise upwards. Yet, they still obey the nature of the universe and submit to being mingled with the body. The earthly and fluid parts of you have a tendency to flow downwards, but they are held up and made to occupy a position that is not natural to them.

Thus, even these elements obey the laws of the universe. When they are assigned a place, they remain there until the universe signals the end and recalls them.

Isn't it strange, then, that only the thinking part is disobedient and discontented with the place assigned to it? It isn't as if something is forced on it, but only what is in accordance with its own nature. Still, it rebels and sets off in the opposite direction. To be drawn towards injustice, indulgence, anger, grief, and fear is a revolt against nature. When the mind is unhappy with anything that happens, it quits its post. It was created to show reverence and piety towards the gods and act justly. These qualities are a part of the fellowship of the universe and a prerequisite for justice.

---

21. Do what is good for the community

The saying that "if you don't have a consistent goal in life, you can't live consistently," is incomplete, unless you add something about the goal. Not everyone agrees on what is good, with the exception of things that affect the welfare of society. So, the goal you propose should benefit your fellow human beings and the community. If you direct your every effort towards that, your actions will be consistent, and you will be consistent.

22. Don't exchange the quiet for the noise

Remember the country mouse and the town mouse and the alarm and agitation of the town mouse.[45]

23. Popular beliefs are 'bogies'

Socrates used to call popular beliefs 'bogies' to scare children.

24. Treat your guests well

At festivals, the Spartans would seat guests in the shade, but they themselves would sit anywhere.

25. On accepting a favour

Socrates declined an invitation to attend the court of Perdiccas because he (Socrates) would die of shame (since he wouldn't be able to return the favour).[46]

26. Use a virtuous life as a model

Epicurean writings offer this advice: You should often think of someone in the past who lived a virtuous life.

27. Stars don't wear veils

The Pythagoreans used to say that you should look up at the sky first thing in the morning to remind ourselves how regularly and punctually these bodies perform their work, how orderly they are, and how pure and transparent they are. Stars don't wear veils.

28. Look at things differently

Think of Socrates dressed in his loincloth when [his wife] Xanthippe had walked off with his cloak. Think of what he said to his friends when they were embarrassed by him and tried to avoid him.[47]

29. Learn the art of living before teaching

You cannot be an instructor if you have not learned to read and write. How much more so in the art of living!

30. Don't be slavish. Be free

You are a slave. Free speech is not for you.

31. And my heart laughed within me

And my heart laughed within me.[48]

32. People mock virtue

They will jeer at virtue with taunts and abuse.[49]

33. For everything, there's a season
The fool looks for figs in winter and children in old age.[50]

34. What is natural is not ominous
Epictetus said, "When you kiss your child, silently say to yourself that tomorrow, perhaps, the child may die."

"These are ominous words," they said.

"Not at all. No natural thing is ominous. Would you say that it is ominous to harvest grains?"

35. Constant changes
Grape – unripe, ripe, raisin. All are changes, not into nothing, but into something that is yet to exist.

36. No one can rob you of your free will
No one can rob us of our free will.[51]

37. Be careful what you assent to
Epictetus also said that we should create a system for giving assent. We should pay attention to our impulses and make sure they are moderated and consistent with social interests, and they have regard for the value of the object. Our desires should be restrained and our aversions should be limited to matters under our control.

38.   Your sanity depends on your assent

Epictetus said the dispute is not is about a trivial thing. It is about sanity.

39. A rational person doesn't quarrel

Socrates asked, "What do you want: a rational or an irrational mind?"

"A rational mind."

"Healthy or sick?"

"Healthy."

"Then why don't you work toward them?"

"Because I already have them?"

"Then why do you fight and squabble?"

BOOK 12

This is Your Moment

It is not clear when Marcus wrote his last book, but clearly, he was very close to his death (or believed he was). He concludes his Meditation with the following thoughts:

> *You've lived as the citizen of this great world-city. What is it to you whether it is five or five score years? The laws of the city are fair for one and all. What is your complaint? ...*
>
> *Make your exit graciously with a smile, with the creator smiling as you exit.*

Gracious words from a gracious emperor.

1. You can have everything right now

You have been trying to reach many things by taking the long way around. All these things can be yours right now if you stop denying them to yourself. All you have to do is let go of the past, trust the future to providence, and direct the present to reverence and justice.

- Reverence is accepting whatever happens to you because nature created and assigned it to you.
- Justice is speaking the truth, frankly and candidly, and having respect for law and the rights of others.

Don't be stopped by other people's misbehaviour, your own misconceptions, or your bodily sensations. The body can take care of itself.

When it is your time to depart, set everything aside, except your mind and the divinity within. Be more concerned that you have never begun to live in accordance with nature than with death. Then you'll become a human being worthy of the universe. You will stop being a stranger in your own homeland, shocked by everyday events as if they are something unexpected. You will stop being dependent on this or that.

---

2. Avoid life's make-believe

God sees our minds free of their bodily containers, stripped of impurities and grime. With his mind, he contacts us only with what has flown and channelled from him. Learn to do the same and you will save yourself a lot of trouble. When you see through the flesh that covers you, will you waste any more time going after fine clothes, houses, and a reputation or any of the rest of life's make-believe?

3. Only your mind is yours

You are made of three parts: body, breath, and mind. The first two are yours only in the sense that you are responsible for their care. The last one alone is fully yours.

If you can separate your mind (which is your true self) from

- everything others do or say,
- everything you have said and done in the past,
- every anxiety about the future,
- everything affecting the body and its partner breath,
- everything that is outside your control, and
- every outward circumstance that swirls around you,

your mind can be free of whatever fate may bring.

If you can cut free impressions that cling to your mind and make yourself, as Empedocles[52] says, 'a sphere enjoying perfect stillness', you can live pure and free, doing what is just, accepting what happens, and speaking the truth.

A well-rounded sphere, rejoicing in its perfect stillness

Live only the life you are living now in the present moment, and you will be able to spend the rest of your days free of all anxieties and in kindness and at peace with the spirit that dwells within you.

4. We value other people's opinions more

This never ceases to amaze me. We love ourselves above all others and yet value our opinions less than that of others.

If a god or a wise teacher told us to think of nothing and have no purpose in our heart without shouting it out right away, we could tolerate it for a single day. That's how much we value other people's opinions rather than our own.

5. Everything, even death, is fair

Is it possible that the gods who have designed everything so well and so kindly have overlooked this one thing – that even the most virtuous of us, those who are close to the gods through their good works and devotion, completely cease to exist forever once they die? That they have no re-birth?

Assuming that this is true, you can be sure that, if a different plan were called for, the gods would have made it. If it was just, if it was possible, and if it had been in accordance with nature, nature would have made it happen. From the fact that it is not so (if it is indeed so), you can be sure that is not meant to be.

Don't you see that you are challenging the gods' fairness by raising this idle question? We wouldn't be arguing with the gods this way unless they were perfectly good and just. And, if that is the case, how could they have carelessly overlooked something that is so unfair in designing the universe?

6. Practice makes the difference

Practice, even when success looks hopeless. The left hand, though not very effective at most things through lack of practice, can guide the reins better than the right because it has had good practice at that.

7. Consider the shortness of life

Consider what you want your body and soul to be like when death overtakes you. Consider the shortness of life, the vastness of time before and after, and the fragility of all material things.

8. Everything depends on how you look at it

Look at the underlying cause of things without their coverings. Think about your intention behind your actions. Understand the essences of pain, pleasure, death, and reputation. Observe how your problems are of your own making and how no one obstructs. Everything depends on how you look at it.

9. Always be ready with your principles

In applying your principles, be a boxer and not a swordsman. The swordsman puts down the sword and has to pick it up again. The boxer is never without his hand, and all he has to do is clench his fist.

10. See the true nature of things

See the true nature of things: matter, form, and purpose.

11. The excellent power of human beings

How excellent is this power that human beings have – to do nothing other than what God wants and accept whatever God sends their way!

12. No one is to blame

You should not blame the gods for what happens in accordance with nature because they do nothing wrong either on purpose or by accident. You should not blame human beings either because they don't do wrong on purpose. Blame no one.

13. Nothing should surprise you

How ridiculous and strange it is to be surprised by anything that happens in life!

14. Your rational mind is always intact

Either there is a fatal need and a law that cannot be violated, or a kind Providence, or chaos without purpose or order.

- If it is restless fate, why struggle against it?
- If it is Providence willing to be merciful, do your best to deserve mercy.
- If it is chaos without order, give thanks that, on this raging sea, you have a rational mind to guide you. If the storm carries you away, let it carry away your body, your breath, and everything else. Your rational mind can never be swept away.

15. Don't let your virtues die before you do

A lamp shines without losing its gleam until it is put out. Should truth, wisdom, and justice within you die before you do?

16. If you are upset, work on yourself

If you get the impression that someone has done something wrong, ask yourself, "How can I be sure that this really was wrong?" Even if it is,

- she may have condemned herself for it (like scratching her own eyes out),
- or expecting a bad person not to harm others is like expecting a fig tree not produce fig juice,

babies not to cry, horses never to neigh, and the other inevitable things not happen. Tell me, what else could they do with their character?

If you are still upset, work on *your* character.

---

17. If it is not right, don't do it

If it is not right, don't do it.

If it is not true, don't say it.

Let your intention be [to keep your impulses under control.[53]]

---

18. Examine everything

Always look at the whole thing. What is making an impression on you? Unpack it. Analyze its cause, its matter, its purpose, and its duration.

---

19. See what is clouding your thoughts

Realize that you have something in you that is more powerful and more miraculous than the things that create emotions and make you dance like a puppet.

What is clouding my thoughts now? Fear? Suspicion? Desire? Something else of that nature?

---

20. Don't act at random without a purpose

First, don't act at random without a purpose. Second, let all your actions be for the common good.

21. All things are born to change

Before long, you will be no one, nowhere. Nothing you see now nor any of the people alive now will exist. All things are born to change, alter, and perish to make room for new things to come.

22. Everything is opinion

Everything is opinion and opinion is in your power. You can take away your opinion any time you choose. Then, like a ship that has passed a rough patch, the sea is calm, still, and there's not a wave in the bay.

23. Death is nothing bad or shameful

Any activity that ends at its proper time – no matter what it is – suffers no harm because it has come to an end. Neither does the person who performed the action and brought it to an end.

Similarly, our life, which is the sum of all actions, suffers no evil because it has come to an end if it is the proper time. The one who brings this about suffers no harm either. The proper hour and limit are fixed by nature – sometimes by our individual nature such as old age, but always the universal nature. She constantly changes her parts and keeps the universe forever young and vigorous.

Now what is good for the whole is kept entirely fair and blooming. It follows then that the end of life is nothing bad or shameful. It not our choice and is not against the common good. It is timely for the universe and benefits it. Following the path of God, thinking His thoughts, is how we become divine.

---

24. Three handy thoughts

Keep these three principles handy.

1. *Your actions and external events.* Never act without a purpose or unjustly. If something happens to you, it happens either by choice or by design. Blame neither choice nor design.

2. *The nature of things.* Think well about what everything is from the time it was a seed, to the birth of a soul, to its end. What are they made of? Where do they return to?

3. *The sameness of things.* Suppose you were suddenly carried up and could look down on the whole set of human activities. You will see a host of beings live around air and ether and view it with contempt. No matter how high you go, you will see the same things being short-lived and changing. And, you are proud of these things!

---

25. Throw away your judgments

Throw away your judgments and you are saved. Who is stopping you from doing this?

26. Things you forgot

When you are troubled by anything, you've forgotten these:

- All things happen according to nature.
- Other people's misbehaviour is nothing to you.
- Whatever happens has always happened, always will happen, and is happening now everywhere.
- The relationship between human beings is very close because it is a community – not of blood or seed, but of intelligence.
- Every human being's intelligence is a god and has flowed from there. Nothing is our very own. Our children, our body, and even our breath have come from there.
- Everything is opinion.
- You can live only in the present moment. You can only lose this.

27. Don't strive for cheap things

Constantly think about those who have felt very upset at something. Those that were most famous. Those that were most unfortunate. Those who faced fame or enmity of any kind. Where are they now? Smoke, ash and a story. Maybe not even a story.

Also, think about everything like this. Fabius and Catullinus lived in the country, Lucius Lupus in his gardens, Stretitinus at Baiae, Tiberius at Capri, and Rufus at Velia. All obsession and arrogance.[54]

How cheap are the things we struggle to get!

How much wiser would it be to accept what we are given and show justice, moderation, and obedience to God, and do this in all simplicity. The most objectionable pride is the one that grows behind the veil of humility.

---

28. Why the gods exist

To those who ask, "Where have you seen the gods?", "What evidence do you have of their existence that you worship them this devoutly?" I say, "First, look around you. They can be seen with your eyes. Second, I haven't seen my soul either, yet I honour it. That's how I know the gods exist. From what I experience of their power in every moment of my life, I know the gods exist and I revere them."

---

29. What else is there but to enjoy life?

For a safe and secure life, develop a thorough insight into things.

- Understand their full nature: what they are made of, what is in their nature.
- Speak what is true with all your heart.

What else is there but to enjoy your life, doing one good act after another with no gap between them?

30. The unity of everything

There is one sunlight, even when it is broken by walls, mountains, and a thousand other things.

- There is one substance, even when it is broken into a thousand forms of life, each with its own special qualities.
- There is one soul, even when it is divided among countless natures in different proportions.
- Even the soul given the gift of thought, even when it looks divisible, is one.
- The other parts – breath, matter – lack sensations and connections to one another, yet even these parts are kept together by gravitational forces.

Intelligence is spontaneously drawn towards anything of its own kind and combines with it, so the feeling of unity is not interrupted.

31. Pursue things that are of value

What do you want? To keep on breathing? Is it to experience sensations, desire, and growth? Is it to use your powers of speech and thought? What is there in any of these that is worth going for?

If you see little value in these things, look at what is left – following reason and God, but remember, to value these other things and feel sad because death will take them.

32. Only following nature's will matters

How small a fraction of the boundless and infinite time is a given to each of us! An instant and it disappears into eternity.

How small a fraction of the whole substance!

How small part of the universal soul!

How small a part of the whole world do you crawl!

As you think on these things, understand that nothing is great, except doing whatever nature demands and accepting whatever nature gives you.

33. Reason is supreme

How does your ruling faculty make use of reason? All depends on this. The rest – whether in your power or not – is just lifeless ashes and smoke.

34.   Look upon death with contempt

Think on this to develop contempt for death: even those who think pleasure is good and pain is bad despise it.

35. Death holds no terror

- When you find your sole good in what happens at the right time,
- when you don't care if your actions are few or many, as they are in accordance with reason, and
- when you don't care if you live long or briefly,

death will hold no terror for you.

36.   Exit with grace

You've lived as a citizen of this great world-city. What is it to you whether it is five or five score years? The laws of the city are fair for one and all. What is your complaint?

You are not thrown out of the city by a tyrant or by an unfair judge, but by nature that brought you here in the first place. Like a director dismisses an actor.

"But I have played only three acts of the five."

"Yes, you say it well, but the play has only three acts in your life."

The completeness of the play is decided by the creator of the play. He decides how it ends. These are not your decisions. Make your exit graciously with a smile, with the creator smiling as you exit

.

NOTES

[1] Robin Hard. (Marcus Aurelius.) *Meditations: With Selected Correspondence*. Oxford University Press, 2011.

[2] Marcus Annius Verus, who adopted Marcus after his father's death.

[3] Also called Marcus Annius Verus who died when Marcus was still a child.

[4] Marcus' wealthy and educated mother, Domitella Lucilla.

[5] Maternal great-grandfather, Lucius Catilius Severus.

[6] Unclear who this might be.

[7] Marcus' painting teacher.

[8] Quintus Junius Rusticus, politician and consul.

[9] Apollonius of Chalcedon, Stoic philosopher and sophist.

[10] Sextus of Chaeronea, Platonist philosophy instructor.

[11] Marcus Cornilius Fronto. Taught.

[12] A philosopher who later served as Marcus' Greek secretary.

[13] Athenodotus is a teacher of Fronto. It is unclear who Domitus was.

[14] These are people who suffered because they lived a principled life: Thrasea Paetus was a Stoic and Nero forced him to kill himself. A man named Helvidius was executed under Vespasian and another, Helvidius, his relative, was executed under Domitian. Cato fought on the Republican side and killed himself rather than

surrender to Julius Caesar. Brutus killed himself soon after Philippi was defeated. Dio tried to improve and replace the rule of the tyrant Dionysius II.

[15] Claudius Maximus, consul, later governor of Africa.

[16] Lucius Verus, adopted by Antonius Pius along with Marcus.

[17] Presumably the names of household slaves with whom sex would have been permissible.

[18] The philosopher who succeeded Aristotle as the head of Lyceum in 322 BC.

[19] Lived in fourth-century BCE.

[20] Well-known tyrants.

[21] 'The universe is change. Life is just opinion,' is from the sayings of Democrates, a 5th Century CE thinker.

[22] This quote implies that we should combine our loyalty to our local (Athenian) and universal city.

[23] Ancient Stoics believed that the particle of divine fire that constitutes the human soul was nourished by blood.

[24] See Book 3.5

[25] Plato, *Republic* 6.486.

[26] Antisthenes.

[27] From *Bellerophon* of Euripides.

[28] From *Hysipyle* of Euripides.

[29] From *Acharnenses* of Aristophanes.

[30] From *Acharnenses* of Aristophanes.

[31] From *Apology*, Plato.

[32] From Plato

[33] *Chrysippus* of Euripides

---

[34] Euripides. Tr. Gregory Hayes

[35] This refers to Socrates' refusal to arrest Leon of Salamis, an honest man, when ordered to do so.

[36] This last paragraph is corrupt, and the meaning is obscure.

[37] Sarmatians are people originally of Iranian stock who migrated from Central Asia to the Ural Mountains between the 6th and 4th century BCE

[38] From Euripidea, Check, Tr. Maxwell Staniforth.

[39] Most names mentioned below refer to obscure individuals. However, it is not necessary to know their identity to follow the points made by Marcus here.

[40] Homer, Iliad VI.146. Translation by George Long.

[41] It is open to question whether the reference to Christians was inserted by others later. In the Loeb edition of *Mediations*, C.R. Haines offers the opinion that this was a later insertion. His reasoning is that the clause "is outside the construction and in fact ungrammatical. It is in the very form of a marginal note, and has every appearance of being a gloss foisted into the text."

[42] Sophocles, *Oedipus the King*. Refers to Oedipus' anguished cry after blinding himself. (Mount Cithaeron was where he was abandoned as a child.)

[43] From Oedipus Rex by Sophocles, as translated by George Long. The terms Old Comedy, Middle Comedy, and New Comedy refer to comedies that arose during different periods before the fourth-century BCE.

[44] Phocion was an Athenian general and statesman. He was accused of treachery by the people and condemned

to die. Yet, before he died, he said, "I have no grudge against the Athenians."

⁴⁵ This is based on a fable for which both Horace's Satires and Aesop's fable 297 are cited as sources. Although the implication is not clear, Maxwell Staniforth suggests that we should not exchange the quiet of our soul for the perturbations of the world.

⁴⁶ Many scholars feel that Marcus Aurelius is mistaken here. The king who invited Socrates to Macedonia was, in fact, the son of Perdiccas, Aarchlaus.

⁴⁷ There is no record of this incident. However, it appears from the context that Socrates would have exhibited his characteristic indifference to social conventions.

⁴⁸ This is a quote from Homer. Its purpose here is not clear.

⁴⁹ Hesiod, Works and Days/

⁵⁰ Epictetus, *Discourses* III.24

⁵¹ Epictetus, *Discourses* III.22

⁵² A Greek pre-Socratic philosopher

⁵³ Some text is missing here.

⁵⁴ All people mentioned are here are obscure characters.

ABOUT THE AUTHOR

Dr. Chuck Chakrapani has been a long-term, but embarrassingly inconsistent, practitioner of Stoicism. He is the president of Leger Analytics, Chief Knowledge Officer of The Blackstone Group in Chicago, and a Distinguished Visiting Professor at Ryerson University.

Chuck has written books on several subjects over the years, which include research methods, statistics, and investment strategies. His personal website is Chuck-Chakrapani.com

His books on Stoicism include *Unshakable Freedom, A Fortunate Storm,* and *The Good Life Handbook* (a rendering of Epictetus' *Enchiridion.*)

ALSO BY THE AUTHOR

Stoicism in Plain English

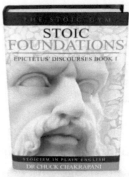

Stoic Foundations is the plain English version of Discourses Book 1 by the eminent Stoic philosopher Epictetus. It revolves around 10 themes, which are also repeated in other places throughout Discourses.

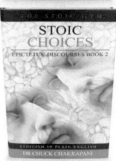

Stoic Choices is the plain English version of Discourses Book 2 by the eminent Stoic philosopher Epictetus. It revolves around themes of choice,, which are also repeated in other places throughout Discourses.

Stoic Training is the third book of *Discourses* of Epictetus in plain English. Stoics did not only believe in theoretical knowledge, but held that it is critical we practice what we learned.

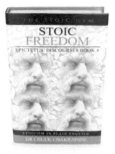

Stoic Freedom is the fourth book of Discourses of Epictetus in plain English. Personal freedom is close to Epictetus' heart, and his rhetoric shines when he talks about freedom. But, what does a free person look like?

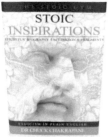

Stoic Inspirations combines the Enchiridion (Epictetus' pupil Arrian's notebook summarizing his teachings) and the remaining fragments of the lost Discourses books. It completes the Stoicism in Plain English series on Epictetus from The Stoic Gym.

Stoicism in Plain English books 1-5 represent the complete works of Epictetus.

Stoic Lessons is the complete works of Musonius Rufus (25-95CE), the man who taught Epictetus. While he was very well-known and respected during his time, he is less widely known now. He was a social activist, a proto-feminist, a vegetarian, and a minimalist.

Get your copies in your favourite online bookstore.

A Fortunate Storm

How did Stoicism come about?

Three unconnected events – a shipwreck in Piraeus, a play in Thebes, and the banishment of a rebel in Turkey – connected three unrelated individuals to give birth to a philosophy. It was to endure for 2,000 years and offered hope and comfort to hundreds of thousands of people along the way. The Fortunate Storm is the improbable story of how Stoicism came about. You can get a FREE COPY of the e-version of this book at TheStoicGym.com/fortunatestormfree

The Good Life Handbook

Available in print, digital, and audio editions, *The Good Life Handbook* is a rendering of *Enchiridion* in plain English. It is a concise summary of the teachings of Epictetus, as transcribed and later summarised by his student, Flavius Arrian.

Now The Stoic Gym offers *The Good Life Handbook* by Dr Chuck Chakrapani to interested readers for FREE (Kindle and other online versions).

Please get your copy in your favourite online bookstore.

Unshakable Freedom

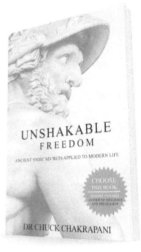

How can we achieve total personal freedom when we have so many obligations and so many demands on our time? Is personal freedom even possible?

Yes, it is possible, said the Stoics, and they gave us a blueprint for freedom. The teachings were lost but have been rediscovered in recent times and form the basis of modern cognitive therapy.

In *Unshakable Freedom*, Dr Chuck Chakrapani outlines the Stoic secrets for achieving total freedom, no matter who you are and what obstacles you face in life.

Using modern examples, Chuck explores how anyone can achieve personal freedom by practising a few mind-training techniques

Get your copy today from all good online bookstores.

Made in United States
Troutdale, OR
11/14/2023

14562667R00137